D1146175

THE BOOK OF CELEBRITY USELESS INFORMATION

THE BOOK OF
CELEBRITY
USELESS
INFORMATION

BY MARK HANKS

JOHN BLAKE

Published by John Blake Publishing Ltd,
3 Bramber Court, 2 Bramber Road,
London W14 9PB, England

www.blake.co.uk

First published in hardback in 2008

ISBN: 978 1 84454 651 0

British Library Cataloguing-in-Publication Data:

A catalogue record for this book is available from the British Library.

Design by www.envydesign.co.uk

Printed and bound in Great Britain by Creative Print & Design. Blaina. Wales.

1 3 5 7 9 10 8 6 4 2

Papers used by John Blake Publishing are natural, recyclable products made from
wood grown in sustainable forests. The manufacturing processes conform to the
environmental regulations of the country of origin.

Every attempt has been made to contact the relevant copyright-holders, but some
were unobtainable. We would be grateful if the appropriate people could contact us.

*With thanks to my favourite Flashman reader
and Rhona Mercer.*

CONTENTS

THE A–Z OF CELEBRITY TRIVIA

★ ★ ★ ★ THE A–Z OF CELEBRITY TRIVIA ★ ★ ★ ★

★ **ABBA** rather imaginatively took the first letter from each of their names – Agnetha, Bjorn, Benny, Ani-frid – to come up with their group name. The group once turned down an offer of £1 billion to reunite.

★ Pop star and *American Idol* judge **Paula Abdul** was once married to Emilio Estevez. She is Jewish.

★ Hollywood actress **Jean Acker** split with her new husband, heartthrob Rudolph Valentino, on their wedding night.

★ Actress **Amy Adam**s worked as a Hooters waitress at the age of 18. 'I did it because I needed to buy a car,' she told the *Mail on Sunday* in 2006. She left Hooters after saving $900 – enough to buy a used Chevrolet. She was raised a Mormon, but departed the religion in her teens.

★ Canadian singer **Bryan Adams** was arrested for pot as a teenager. Years later he was nearly killed during a parachute jump.

★ *Paycheck* star **Ben Affleck** caught the acting bug early on, appearing in ads for Burger King. When he was little, he asked his mum for a dog and she tested him by making him walk an imaginary pup for a week. In

★ ★ ★ ★ THE A–Z OF CELEBRITY TRIVIA ★ ★ ★ ★

the end, he only lasted five days and didn't get the dog. Ben was an extra in the *Buffy the Vampire* film in 1992 and both he and fellow *Good Will Hunting* star Matt Damon were extras in the 1989 film *Field of Dreams*, starring Kevin Costner. Ben auditioned for the part of Les Anderson in *License to Drive*, which went to Corey Haim. When Ben was directing *Gone Baby Gone*, Boston police mistook him for a drug dealer and he, along with some of the crew, were almost arrested. When he was dating Jennifer Lopez, the high-profile couple was known as 'Bennifer'. Ben and wife Jennifer Garner are known as 'Bennifer Part II'. He owns a vintage Pacman arcade game.

★ Though pop singer and songwriter **Christina Aguilera** is of Ecuadorian descent and recorded an album in Spanish, she doesn't speak the language. She hired French designer Christian Lacroix to make her wedding dress. When Christina was a member of *The New Mickey Mouse Club* in the mid-90s, the other members nicknamed her 'Diva'. She once paid a trip to hospital after a plant fell on her head, and she sometimes sleeps with a night light. Aguilera has earned five Grammy Awards and 18 nominations. She sang 'The Star-Spangled Banner' before Pittsburgh Penguins and the Pittsburgh Steelers ice hockey matches in her teens. Aguilera is involved with several

★ ★ ★ ★ THE A-Z OF CELEBRITY TRIVIA ★ ★ ★ ★

charities and petitioned the South Korean government for the country to stop the alleged killing of dogs for food. She also supports Women's Center & Shelter of Greater Pittsburgh and donated $200,000 to the shelter. Apparently, Christina and her husband like being nude on Sundays to keep the marriage alive.

★ The bra that **Jessica Alba** wore in *Sin City* got a bid of a whopping $1,025 on eBay in 2007. She was 'sex star of the year' in *Playboy* Magazine in 2006, and named as having the most kissable celebrity lips in a poll conducted by Colgate. She auditioned for the part of Elektra in *Daredevil*, a role which ended up going to Jennifer Garner. Her nickname is Sky Angel and she loves playing golf. When she was a child, Jessica's lungs collapsed twice and she was unlucky enough to get pneumonia a few times a year. She loves Harley Davidsons, and her fans bought 50,000 Jessica Alba *Dark Angel* action figures when they were released.

★ Blur frontman **Damon Albarn** was bullied at school because other kids thought he was a 'gayboy'.

★ Boxing legend **Muhammad Ali** met Sonji Roi in 1964 and asked her to marry him that day. She said yes, and they were hitched within six weeks.

★ ★ ★ ★ THE A–Z OF CELEBRITY TRIVIA ★ ★ ★ ★

★ Singer **Lily Allen** used to deal drugs as a teenager, but admits she would use more than she would sell. In January 2007, Lily was reunited with her English bull terrier, Maggie May, who was stolen from a friend's van just before New Year. Lily is the daughter of actor and musician Keith Allen, and her mother dated comedian Harry Enfield, with whom they both lived for a time. By the age of 17, Lily was already a member of London's exclusive Groucho Club. At one stage, the singer studied horticulture with the intention of becoming a florist, but soon returned to music.

★ *Home Improvement*'s **Tim Allen** spent two years in jail (1978–80) on drug-dealing charges. During the last season of the show, he took home $1.25 million per episode.

★ *Cheers* actress **Kirstie Alley** is scared of flying.

★ *Never Mind the Buzzcocks* presenter **Simon Amstell** is also a stand-up comedian. He co-wrote an episode of popular teen drama programme *Skins*.

★ The name **Anastacia** is Greek for 'She who will rise again'. Before she was famous, every music-business person she met told her to get contact lenses if she wanted to succeed. Now her glasses have become her trademark.

★ ★ ★ ★ THE A-Z OF CELEBRITY TRIVIA ★ ★ ★ ★

★ *X-files* star **Gillian Anderson** was bullied at school because of her independent and bossy attitude. She was voted 'Most Likely to Go Bald and Most Likely to Be Arrested' when she was at school. Gillian once went diving with sharks, an experience she found breathtaking, exciting, frightening and liberating.

★ Former *Baywatch* babe **Pamela Anderson** was born on 1 July 1967, in British Columbia, Canada, to Barry, a furnace repair man, and waitress Carol. Pamela made headlines right from the start by being the first baby of Canada's centennial year. She grew up naturally sporty, with her athleticism earning her the nickname 'Rubber Band' at school. In Vancouver, aged 22, at a Canadian Football League game, Pammy was caught on the stadium's big screen by a cameraman during a break in play, and her fame began there. Pamela passed her driving test at the fourth attempt. She failed her first test for hitting another car. She also vows that she will never have a facelift and keeps nasty emails from ex-boyfriends so she can remind herself that the men in her life often make her think they love her when they don't.

★ Former model and *I'm a Celebrity … Get Me Out of Here!* contestant **Sophie Anderton**'s 1996 advert for Gossard attracted a record number of complaints to the

★ ★ ★ ★ THE A-Z OF CELEBRITY TRIVIA ★ ★ ★ ★

Advertising Standards Authority. When she was on ITV's *Love Island*, the show's presenters Fearne Cotton and Patrick Kielty called her 'Me Me'. She was nicknamed Thunder-thighs at school.

★ OutKast star **André 3000** is vegan. He was voted the world's sexiest male vegetarian celebrity by PETA (People for the Ethical Treatment of Animals).

★ *Friends* star **Jennifer Aniston** had the same thing for lunch for nine years. The Groundhog Day lunch in question: lettuce, garbanzo beans, turkey and lemon dressing. In 1980 her parents divorced and Jennifer lived mainly with her mother Nancy, although the two fell out after Nancy appeared on US television to talk about her famous daughter. 'I will *never* forgive you,' Jennifer apparently told her mother.

Jennifer has said that yoga helped her deal with her split from Brad Pitt. After their split she took his clothes to a charity shop. Jennifer is a sleepwalker but doesn't tend to remember her nighttime adventures. The *Guinness World Book of Records 2005* documents that Jen and fellow *Friends* actors were paid $1 million-per-episode in the tenth series of the programme. She has had her artwork exhibited at New York's Metropolitan Museum of Art. Her godfather was the late actor Teddy Savalas.

★ ★ ★ ★ THE A-Z OF CELEBRITY TRIVIA ★ ★ ★ ★

★ TV presenters **Ant and Dec** – Geordie duo Anthony McPartlin and Declan Donnelly – have admitted they didn't hit it off straight away. 'We didn't particularly like each other at first, I thought he was miserable,' said Dec. 'We've rowed a few times – we're quite competitive,' said Ant. Ant is scared of spiders and Dec is afraid of pigeons.

★ US actress **Christina Applegate** has tattoos on her left and right ankles. One says 'Nini' (her mum's nickname) and the other says 'Agape' (Greek for unconditional love).

★ All Saint **Natalie Appleton** has a child called Ace Billy Howlett with Prodigy star Liam Howlett. She appeared in *Grange Hill* in 1986. She was on *I'm a Celebrity … Get me Out of Here!* in 2004 but lasted just a week before quitting.

★ **Nicole Appleton** was suspended from school for stealing crisps from a classmate. The crisps in question were Wotsits, and her orange fingers gave the game away. She has a son called Gene with Oasis frontman Liam Gallagher. She appeared in 2000 film *Honest*, in which both she and fellow All Saint and sister Natalie did nude scenes together. Aside from Natalie, she has two other sisters – Lori and Lee.

★ ★ ★ ★ THE A-Z OF CELEBRITY TRIVIA ★ ★ ★ ★

★ *Spitting Image* once received a recording from disgraced author **Jeffrey Archer** so that they could do a better job of impersonating him.

★ Hollywood dancing legend **Fred Astaire** had his legs insured for £53,000, but his dancing partner Cyd Charise had hers covered for a more impressive £3.5 million.

★ Blues Brother **Dan Aykroyd**'s conehead from *Saturday Night Live* was sold off at auction for £1,500.

★ As a youngster, a wannabe pop star frequently skipped school to attend auditions and dance rehearsals. Eventually she would become **Mel B**.

★ **Kevin Bacon** doesn't watch films he starred in when he was younger because he says he can only see faults in his performances. He never met his co-stars Robert De Niro and Dustin Hoffman during the production of *Sleepers*. Kevin is the subject of a game called 'Six Degrees of Kevin Bacon', in which players have to link any actor to Kevin Bacon in the fewest links possible. Kevin is in a band with his brother Michael called The Bacon Brothers. They have released five albums.

★★★★ THE A-Z OF CELEBRITY TRIVIA ★★★★

★ Hollywood actor **Alec Baldwin** once failed an audition to play himself when he offered to voice his own puppet in *Team America: World Police* and was turned down.

★ Batman **Christian Bale** ate live maggots for his role as Dieter Dengler in the film *Rescue Dawn*. He played the only American ever to escape from a Prisoner of War camp.

★ TV star and DJ **Zoe Ball**'s dad is former children's television presenter Johnny Ball. Her first ever record purchase was Slade's 'Merry Xmas Everybody'.

★ *America's Next Top Model* presenter **Tyra Banks**, at the age of 23, was the first black model ever to appear on the cover of *Sports Illustrated*'s famous Swimsuit Issue. Tyra is afraid of dolphins.

★ Television presenter **Sue Barker** once had to shell out £7,000 on repairs to her Ferrari caused by … a mouse.

★ US comedian and TV host **Roseanne Barr** was once an opening act for Julio Iglesias.

★ **Julian Barratt**, who stars in the comedy series *The Mighty Boosh*, dislikes appearing in television comedy

★ ★ ★ ★ THE A-Z OF CELEBRITY TRIVIA ★ ★ ★ ★

quiz shows. The comedian would 'rather be at home with a book'.

★ **Drew Barrymore**'s godfather is none other than Steven Spielberg. He made her a star in *ET* and three years later she starred in Stephen King's *Cat's Eye* – a part written specifically for her. After she posed for *Playboy* in 1995, Spielberg sent a note that said 'cover yourself up' along with a quilt and a copy of the magazine with all her pictures altered so that she appeared fully clothed.

★ Comedian and TV presenter **Michael Barrymore** used to cut hair for Vidal Sassoon.

★ **Mischa Barton** was the second actor cast for *The OC*. The first was Peter Gallagher. She has two dogs named Ziggy Stardust and Charlie Barton. Miss Barton does not have her own stylist and her favourite movies are *Say Anything*, *Almost Famous*, *The Godfather* and *The Graduate*. Clotheswise, her style icons are Cate Blanchett, Kate Beckinsale, Gwyneth Paltrow and Cameron Diaz. She is obsessed with socks, especially stripy ones, and loves to eat chocolate and sushi, though presumably not at the same time.

★ ★ ★ ★ THE A-Z OF CELEBRITY TRIVIA ★ ★ ★ ★

★ *9½ Weeks* star **Kim Basinger** was Miss Junior Athens in 1969. She is a collector of inflatable ducks. Before she received therapy for it, Kim's agoraphobia could keep her housebound for up to six months at a time. As a child, she suffered from crippling shyness which stopped her from reading aloud or speaking in class.

★ Welsh diva **Dame Shirley Bassey** once had a job packing up chamber pots. She would write her name and address on them and says she received replies from around the world. Dame Shirley is the first singer to have been invited to record more than one James Bond theme tune. She was invited to sing at John F Kennedy's Inauguration Ball at the White House and also lived in Switzerland for two years as a tax exile.

★ TV prankster **Jeremy Beadle** was the first person in Britain to bag a video phone.

★ *Lord of the Rings* and *Bravo Two Zero* star **Sean Bean** used to dye his hair and wear make-up.

★ **David Beckham** was discovered to have one leg shorter than the other during his medical for Spanish club Real Madrid. He has wife Victoria's name in Hindi tattooed on his arm. It is spelled incorrectly.

★ ★ ★ ★ THE A-Z OF CELEBRITY TRIVIA ★ ★ ★ ★

David insisted on wearing a Red Devils shirt when training with London club Tottenham Hotspur as a schoolboy. David's legs are insured for $70 million.

★ **Victoria Beckham** admits to having wanted to be a star from the age of eight, after seeing the film *Fame*. Posh had a cameo role in *Ugly Betty*. She was the only band member who didn't sing a solo on the 2007 Spice Girls comeback tour. Posh and Becks' joint wealth is estimated to be over £110 million. Around £1 million was paid for serialisation rights to Victoria's book *Learning to Fly*. For their wedding they hired over 430 employees.

★ British actress **Kate Beckinsale** lives in Venice, California, because she says it reminds her of London. She won WH Smith's Young Writers' competition two years running, once for her short stories and the other time for poetry. She studied French and Russian literature at Oxford University. PE was her least favourite subject at school. Not a fan of gratuitous nude scenes, Kate once urinated into the Thermos of a director who pushed her into doing a nude scene.

★ It-girl **Tamara Beckwith** agreed to leave Cheltenham Ladies College for good after she turned up to school as a punk.

★ ★ ★ ★ THE A-Z OF CELEBRITY TRIVIA ★ ★ ★ ★

★ Recording artist **Daniel Bedingfield** wrote his hit 'Gotta Get Thru This' at the age of 18, just two years after getting his first synthesiser. The pride he takes in the success of the single barely compares to the knowledge that it's Victoria Beckham's favourite song. In 2004 he broke his neck in an accident and was very lucky to survive.

★ Pop star **Natasha Bedingfield** studied psychology at the University of Greenwich for a year to make her a better songwriter. She wrote her first song at the age of 12. Sylvester Stallone approached her at a Hollywood party to record the theme tune for the last Rocky film, *Rocky Balboa*. The song was never used. She was once in a group with brother Daniel called DNA Algorithm.

★ According to her mother, *Forgetting Sarah Marshall* star **Kristen Bell** used to drag her bowl to the floor and eat next to the dog dish at the age of four. Kristen sometimes collects stray animals and offers them shelter in her house.

★ Sultry Italian star **Monica Bellucci** was studying law before she became a model and then an actress.

★ Wacky movie star **Roberto Benigni** was the first actor to win a Best Actor Oscar for a non-English

★ ★ ★ ★ THE A-Z OF CELEBRITY TRIVIA ★ ★ ★ ★

speaking role. He also achieved a similar 'distinction' when he repeated the feat for the Worst Actor at the Razzies – the anti-Oscars, celebrating the worst of Hollywood for the year.

★ Veteran American crooner **Tony Bennett** was an infantryman with the US Army during World War II.

★ Legendary musician **Chuck Berry** once opened a restaurant called the Southern Air in Missouri. According to a former waitress, Berry wired the women's lavatory with a video camera and recorded some 200 unsuspecting patrons using the toilet, among them three minors. Though the state attorney general intervened, charges were dropped when Berry agreed to financially compensate the victims of his 'potty cam'.

★ Hollywood beauty **Halle Berry** appeared for the final curtain call on *Saturday Night Live* with her boots on the wrong feet. The star has also confessed that drinking protein drinks to enhance her muscles for a role caused her to break wind a lot. Halle used to date New Kid on the Block Danny Wood. They broke up because the band thought she was a groupie. One of Halle's unidentified boyfriends was so violent that he dealt her a blow to her ear which left her partially deaf.

★ ★ ★ ★ THE A-Z OF CELEBRITY TRIVIA ★ ★ ★ ★

Halle says she uses a pair of jeans she wore as a teenager to stay in shape, and that when she was young she dreamed of a pill that would make her white.

★ Football legend **George Best** owned two nightclubs in Manchester during the 1960s called Oscar's and Slack Alice's.

★ George Best's son **Calum Best** appeared in both series of ITV's *Love Island* programme. It proved to be second time lucky as he won the second series.

★ British actor **Paul Bettany**'s favourite foods are cheese and broccoli.

★ Pop star **Sophie Ellis-Bextor**'s mother is former *Blue Peter* presenter Janet Ellis.

★ Actress **Jessica Biel**, girlfriend to Justin Timberlake, collects vintage sunglasses with no lenses. She has hazel-coloured eyes.

★ **Rachel Bilson** is half Filipina and half Latina, collects vintage shoes and once starred in a TV commercial for Subway. *The O.C.* actress wanted to be a pre-school teacher before she got into acting. She is afraid of Beagles.

★ ★ ★ ★ THE A–Z OF CELEBRITY TRIVIA ★ ★ ★ ★

★ *American Beauty* star **Thora Birch**'s mum acted in 21 adult films including *Deep Throat* under the name Carol Connors before retiring in 1993.

★ Quirky pop pixie **Björk**'s favourite animal is a polar bear. In recognition of her contribution to promoting Iceland around the world, Iceland's government gave her an island off the coast of her home country.

★ Scouse singer and TV presenter **Cilla Black** was told she was 'suitable for office work' in her final school report.

★ Comic actor **Jack Black** is the son of rocket scientists. His mother worked on the Hubble telescope, and his father worked on 'some stuff that I can't tell you about', Jack says.

★ British actress **Honor Blackman** once knocked out professional wrestler Jackie Pallo during rehearsals for the TV show *The Avengers*.

★ Comedian and actor **Richard Blackwood**'s dad was once married to supermodel Naomi Campbell's mum.

★ After 44 days locked in a plastic box without food, US magician **David Blaine**'s first meal was a plate of

★ ★ ★ ★ THE A-Z OF CELEBRITY TRIVIA ★ ★ ★ ★

chicken satay followed by a big helping of dessert. David opted to do his fast-in-a-box over the River Thames for 44 days because the number matches his birthday, 4 April.

★ Ex-Prime Minister **Tony Blair** was called 'the most difficult boy I ever had to deal with' by his school housemaster. His university band was called The Ugly Rumours.

★ Australian actress **Cate Blanchett** craved sardines when she was pregnant. Cate accepted the part in the *Lord of the Rings* trilogy because she always wanted to wear pointed ears in a film. She wears a size-six shoe.

★ All Saint **Melanie Blatt** went to the Sylvia Young Theatre School, where she met Nicole Appleton. She also appeared in the film *Honest* alongside the Appleton sisters. Her daughter's name is Lilyella and Melanie's middle name is Ruth.

★ R&B diva **Mary J Blige** once had Spider-Man creator Stan Lee help create a superhero cartoon about herself.

★ A broken skull (three times), broken legs, a finger, a rib, a toe, an arm, a wrist, nose and back – **Orlando**

★ ★ ★ ★ THE A-Z OF CELEBRITY TRIVIA ★ ★ ★ ★

Bloom's roll call of injuries throughout his life. Orlando fell off his horse and broke one of his ribs while filming *Lord of the Rings*. His friends call him OB or Orli for short. His first job was as a clay pigeon trapper at a shooting range, he speaks French and he has a dog called Maude. In 2004, Orlando committed himself to Buddhism in an hour-long ceremony in Britain. He learned to surf during the filming of the *Lord of the Rings* trilogy in New Zealand. Archery schools reported an increase in demand following the release of the films, which was attributed to Orlando's character.

★ Acting, and adopting new accents, helped *The Devil Wears Prada* actress **Emily Blunt** overcome a serious speech impediment. She is not related to James Blunt.

★ In June 2007, a poll showed **James Blunt**'s single 'You're Beautiful' to be the most irritating song of all time. Yet, the *Sun* has since revealed that the song has taken the place of Robbie Williams's 'Angels' as a wedding favourite in the UK.

★ **Jon Bon Jovi** turned down the lead role in the film *Footloose*, giving Jon a quick link for the game 'Six Degrees of Kevin Bacon', as Kevin subsequently took the role.

★ ★ ★ ★ THE A–Z OF CELEBRITY TRIVIA ★ ★ ★ ★

★ In 2006, kooky actress **Helena Bonham Carter** bought a $3.5 million mansion once owned by her great-grandfather, former British Prime Minister Herbert Asquith. Helena has her own fashion line called The Pantaloonies. She has admitted to using the F-Word a lot and likes arm-wrestling.

★ U2 singer **Bono**'s real name is Paul Hewson. He took his name from *Bonavox*, a latin phrase meaning 'good voice'. It is said a friend nicknamed him 'Bono Vox' after a hearing-aid shop they regularly passed in Dublin because he sang so loudly he seemed to be singing for the deaf. Bono disliked the name at first. However, on discovering its meaning, he accepted it and shortened it to Bono.

★ Actress **Kate Bosworth**'s eyes are two different colours: hazel and blue. She is a champion equestrian and fluent in Spanish. She used a family Christmas card photo as her headshot for the audition of her breakthrough movie *The Horse Whisperer*. She performed many of her own stunts in *Superman Returns*.

★ On his first day of kindergarten, **David Bowie** was so nervous that he wet himself. He is also afraid of spiders and flying, but these days he manages to hold his bladder when facing his phobias. David has admitted

★ ★ ★ ★ THE A-Z OF CELEBRITY TRIVIA ★ ★ ★ ★

that his claim to be bisexual was really a sham. He made the story up to create more mystery about himself in the 1970s.

★ **Boy George** was expelled from school for bunking off and not doing any work. He was fired from a job in a supermarket for choosing to wear the store's carrier bags.

★ Actress **Lara Flynn Boyle**'s identity was stolen when her Beverly Hills home was robbed and the thief opened accounts in her name. She used to date Jack Nicholson and is dyslexic.

★ **Kenneth Branagh** grew up in poverty in the shadow of a tobacco factory in Belfast. The actor and director has an honorary doctorate from the University of Belfast.

★ Comedian **Russell Brand** used to be a postman. His phobias are death and growing old, but when he does die he would like the song 'Asleep' by The Smiths played at his funeral. At 15 years old, Brand first took to the stage as Fat Sam in *Bugsy Malone*. Everyone who had added Brand as a friend on MySpace was treated to a private stand-up show in 2006. His cat is named after his favourite singer-frontman Morrissey. He practises Capoeira and is a fan of West Ham United FC.

★ ★ ★ ★ THE A-Z OF CELEBRITY TRIVIA ★ ★ ★ ★

★ Godfather **Marlon Brando** was one of several who auditioned for the role of Jay Gatsby in *The Great Gatsby* but lost out to Robert Redford.

★ Former Tory MP **Gyles Brandreth** loved travelling on the tube when young. The broadcaster and writer would revise for school exams while on the Circle Line, getting off each time he got to Paddington so he could go for a cup of tea.

★ Virgin founder **Richard Branson** attended Stowe School, the same school as jazz legend George Melly. As he left school, his headmaster said, 'I predict you will either go to prison or become a millionaire.'

★ **Benjamin Bratt** takes three showers a day. The actor likes to smell clean but doesn't wear cologne.

★ **Jeff Bridges** was considered for the part of Travis Bickle in *Taxi Driver*. In *The Big Lebowski*, Bridges's character the Dude's shirt with Oriental characters and an Asian holding a baseball bat is the same shirt he wears in *The Fisher King*.

★ **Fern Britton** is the daughter of actor Tony Britton. *This Morning* presenter Fern has twin sons called Jack and Harry, as well as two daughters called Gracie and

★ ★ ★ ★ THE A-Z OF CELEBRITY TRIVIA ★ ★ ★ ★

Winnie. She was voted the UK's most big and beautiful celebrity in the *Sun* in April 2007. She has admitted to having gastric band surgery and is married to celebrity chef Phil Vickery.

★ Actor **Jim Broadbent** was offered the part of Del Boy in British sitcom *Only Fools and Horses*, but declined the role, although he guest-starred in three episodes of the show.

★ *Ferris Bueller's Day Off* actor **Matthew Broderick** is allergic to horses. At her 40th birthday, he sang 'I Can Only Give You Love' for wife Sarah Jessica Parker.

★ **Adam Brody**'s favourite food is The Matt Miller sandwich at Canter's Deli in Los Angeles. He became interested in acting while working at Blockbuster Video and went on to become the youngest actor ever to win an Oscar for *The Pianist* in 2003. In 2007, Brody narrowly escaped death when he nearly crashed into a cow while speeding on a highway in India.

★ While filming an underwater scene for the movie *Fishtales*, model and actress **Kelly Brook** hit her head on a submerged pillar. She couldn't swim to safety because her legs were strapped into a mermaid costume. She had to be rescued by divers.

★ ★ ★ ★ THE A-Z OF CELEBRITY TRIVIA ★ ★ ★ ★

★ Irish-born **Pierce Brosnan** entered show business as a teen runaway, working with the circus as a fire eater. Years later, he purchased the typewriter of James Bond creator Ian Fleming for £52,800. He was favoured to replace Roger Moore as James Bond in 1986. However, his contractual obligations to US television programme *Remington Steele* saw Timothy Dalton land the role. Pierce finally got the part in 1995's *Goldeneye*.

★ **Yul Brynner**, famously bald star of *The King and I* and *Westworld*, once worked in the circus as a trapeze artist.

★ US actress **Sandra Bullock** was bullied at school because she was classed as ugly, but she was also voted 'Most Likely to Brighten your Day'. Sandra auditioned for a part in *Runaway Bride*, but lost out to Julia Roberts. She stopped shooting a scene for *Miss Congeniality 2* at the Venetian hotel in Las Vegas to allow newlyweds Diane and Ed Grambo to travel through the set to their reception. Sandra and her husband adopted two dogs, both with missing legs. Sandra uses haemorrhoid cream on her face and is allergic to horses.

★ Model **Gisele Bundchen** wears a size-seven shoe.

★ Spice Girl **Emma Bunton** landed small roles in *The Bill* and *EastEnders*, making it down to the last six for

★ ★ ★ ★ **THE A-Z OF CELEBRITY TRIVIA** ★ ★ ★ ★

the role of Bianca in the latter, a part which eventually went to Patsy Palmer. She was born in North London to a milkman dad and karate instructor mum, and Emma has a Blue Belt in karate. Her greatest fears are going to prison and being alone.

★ *Gimme Gimme Gimme* actress **Kathy Burke** was a foster child.

★ After being twice listed on *Forbes'* Celebrity 100 list, starlet **Amanda Bynes** was given the nickname '99' by her friends, reflecting the star of *Hairspray*'s rank on the list in 2005.

★ As a schoolgirl, Spice Girl **Mel C** used to run for Cheshire county.

★ **Nicolas Cage** started life as Nicholas Coppola, but changed it to disassociate himself from his uncle, famous film director Uncle Francis Ford Coppola. The name 'Cage' came from the comic book character 'Luke Cage'. He was turned down for the role of John Bender in *The Breakfast Club*.

★ Former TV *Superman* **Dean Cain** signed for American football team the Buffalo Bills after leaving university, but a knee injury saw him turn to acting before he'd even played a game.

★ ★ ★ ★ THE A–Z OF CELEBRITY TRIVIA ★ ★ ★ ★

★ As a child, **Michael Caine** had puffy eyes due to blefaritis, bow legs and a nervous jerk called 'Saint Vitus Dance'. His ears protruded badly and his mother used to stick them back with plasters. Eventually, his ears were so close to his head that he would be slightly deaf for the rest of his life. The screen legend took a shine to Shakira Baksh when he saw her in a Maxwell House coffee advert. He was eventually married to her.

★ Supermodel **Naomi Campbell** was born to an 18-year-old unmarried showgirl, and neither Campbell nor her mother has ever publicly named her father. Naomi was the first black model to grace the cover of the French edition of *Vogue*. She was once rescued by police when 4,000 men invaded the beach while she was on holiday in Italy. Naomi starred in Bob Marley and the Wailers' music video for the song 'Is This Love' when she was just seven years old. Nowadays, the supermodel buys new eyelash extensions every six weeks, spending four hours in a specialist London salon. Naomi has no connection with Campbell's soup.

★ **Neve Campbell** suffered a nervous breakdown when she was 14. The star of the *Scream* films lost all of her hair, then underwent acupuncture treatments to help grow it back. She is extremely ticklish especially under her right shoulder blade.

★ ★ ★ ★ THE A-Z OF CELEBRITY TRIVIA ★ ★ ★ ★

★ Former lads' mag favourite **Caprice** once came 120th out of 700 in the World Poker Championship in Los Angeles, beating the likes of actor Ben Affleck in the process. Caprice has a very successful lingerie business under her name.

★ Star of the American version of *The Office* **Steve Carell** originally wanted to be a lawyer, but he reached a question on an application form that asked him why and he couldn't think of an answer, so gave up the idea.

★ Diva **Mariah Carey** was nicknamed 'Mirage' in high school because she never showed up for class. She insured her legs for a billion dollars.

★ **Karen Carpenter** had a doorbell that chimed the start of The Carpenters' hit song 'We've Only Just Begun'.

★ Comedian and TV presenter **Alan Carr** debuted as the Milky Bar Kid aged eight. His father is former footballer Graham Carr. A favourite catchphrase is 'Not My Words', which he uses after making fun of somebody. He is not related to Jimmy Carr.

★ As a child, **Jim Carrey** wore his tap shoes to bed in case his parents needed cheering up in the night. The scene in *The Mask* where he is being chased by

★ ★ ★ ★ THE A–Z OF CELEBRITY TRIVIA ★ ★ ★ ★

gangsters, pulls a wet condom out of his pocket and says, 'Sorry, wrong pocket,' was improvised by Carrey. Jim was in the same acting class as American comedienne Ellen DeGeneres, and his middle name is Eugene. He auditioned for the part of Howard Hughes in *The Aviator*, which eventually went to Leonardo DiCaprio. Jim also lost out to Johnny Depp for *Willy Wonka*.

★ Actor and musician **Aaron Carter** was pulled over by police for speeding before less than 2 ounces of marijuana were found in his car in 2008.

★ Former Cuban leader **Fidel Castro** was a star baseball player for the University of Havana in his youth.

★ *Sex and the City*'s **Kim Cattrall** has said she prefers dating younger guys because men her own age 'can't always keep up'. Kim was born in Liverpool but emigrated with her family to Canada when she was just one year old. She can speak German fluently.

★ Rapper **50 Cent** owns the largest mansion in Connecticut, which boasts 18 bedrooms, 38 bathrooms and a manmade waterfall. Its previous owner was Mike Tyson. 50 Cent and Eminem provided a refreshing change to the usual rider requests at the MTV Music

★ ★ ★ ★ **THE A-Z OF CELEBRITY TRIVIA** ★ ★ ★ ★

Video Awards when they requested four boxes of Kentucky Fried Chicken and Mexican food from Taco Bell.

★ *Mean Girls* actress **Lacey Chabert** was named by her grandmother when she came home from the hospital. Her parents thought they were having a boy and had no idea for a girl's name. Grandma commented on the baby's lacy dress and Lacey's mum liked it.

★ **Jackie Chan** has broken his nose three times, his ankle once, most of the fingers in his hand, both cheekbones and his skull, as well as having a permanent hole in his head from doing stunts on his films. The action-movie star does the dubbing for the English version of his films himself.

★ Silent-movie legend **Charlie Chaplin** got a head start on most people in show business – he started his career at the age of *five*. During a visit to London at the height of his fame, he received 73,000 letters from fans in just two days.

★ **Chevy Chase** featured in the video for 'You Can Call Me Al' by Paul Simon. The American comedian and actor was nearly electrocuted to death during the filming of *Modern Problems* when, during the sequence

★ ★ ★ ★ THE A–Z OF CELEBRITY TRIVIA ★ ★ ★ ★

in which he is wearing landing lights as he dreams that he is an airplane, the current in the lights short-circuited through his arm, back and neck muscles. The near-death experience caused him to experience a period of deep depression.

★ Actress **Kristin Chenoweth** is a trained opera singer with near perfect pitch. She has a dog named Maddie, named after actress Madeline Kahn.

★ Cher's real name is **Cherilyn la Pierre**. She was diagnosed with dyslexia at the age of 30. She is the only certified female performer in music history to have had a US number-one single in the 1960s, 1970s, 1980s and 1990s. She wears size-eight shoes. Cher still can't bring herself to watch *Thelma and Louise* after turning down the Geena Davis role. Her parents married and divorced each other three times.

★ In her days presenting *Popworld*, It-girl **Alexa Chung** once asked Gwen Stefani whether her new brand of perfume would smell like bacon.

★ Welsh singer and television presenter **Charlotte Church** hates her legs because she thinks they look like vases. When she met President George Bush Jr. she told him she was from Wales. He asked her in which state

★ ★ ★ ★ **THE A-Z OF CELEBRITY TRIVIA** ★ ★ ★ ★

Wales lies. Charlotte only got £50 per week until her 18th birthday, despite having a personal fortune in excess of £10 million pounds. She has confessed to spending over £3000 on a dress.

★ **Sir Winston Churchill** smoked an estimated 300,000 cigars in his lifetime.

★ **Eric Clapton** owns one-fifth of the planet Mars. The musician grew up with his grandmother and her second husband and believed they were his parents and that his mother was his older sister. He never knew his real father.

★ *Top Gear*'s **Jeremy Clarkson**'s mother set up a business making Paddington Bear toys in order to make money to give Jeremy a good education. The profits funded Jeremy's place at Repton School. However, Jeremy was asked to leave for inappropriate behaviour including drinking, smoking and seducing girls. He left school with no A-levels.

★ Camp comedian and writer **Julian Clary** once worked as a singing telegram.

★ Comedian **John Cleese**'s father's name was Reg Cleese but his grandfather was named John Edwin Cheese.

★ ★ ★ ★ THE A–Z OF CELEBRITY TRIVIA ★ ★ ★ ★

He changed his name when he joined the British army in 1915.

★ **Bill Clinton** was the first left-handed American president to serve two terms. Clinton only sent two emails during the entire eight years of his presidency. One was to John Glenn in a space shuttle and the other was to test the email system.

★ **Chelsea Clinton** was named after the song 'Chelsea Morning'. As a teenager she became a vegetarian, dreamed of being a paediatric cardiologist and reportedly earned the Secret Service code name 'Energy'.

★ **George Clooney** sometimes sleeps in the walk-in closet of his LA mansion because, he says, 'all the bedrooms are too light'. The *Ocean's Eleven* star defines his perfect woman as a woman who has the laughter of Nicole Kidman, the personality of Julia Roberts, the 'quintessence of beauty' of Michelle Pfeiffer and the ambition of Jennifer Lopez. He is one of only two men to have graced the cover of *Vogue* magazine. The other was Richard Gere. George bought some of Lucy Liu's art from her when she appeared with him on *ER*. George's middle name is Timothy and he once attempted to get into the Cincinnati Reds baseball team in his youth.

★ ★ ★ ★ THE A-Z OF CELEBRITY TRIVIA ★ ★ ★ ★

★ Former Man Behaving Badly **Martin Clunes** is petrified of heights.

★ **Coldplay** really like to live the life of a rock'n'roll band when they tour. Their rider includes a request for eight stamped, local postcards.

★ *Strictly Come Dancing* star **Brendan Cole** has been dancing since the age of six, though he didn't find his dancing skills of much use when he worked as a builder. He won the first series of *Strictly Come Dancing* with dancing partner Natasha Kaplinsky. The pair became partners on and off the dance floor. He has also appeared on *Celebrity Love Island*.

★ Girls Aloud star **Cheryl Cole** was working as a waitress when she entered *Popstars: The Rivals*. Her favourite film is *Ghost* and her favourite actor is 'Gorgeous' George Clooney. Lilly Allen recorded a song – 'Cheryl Tweedy' – about Cheryl. As a child she won Boots the chemist's 'bonniest baby'; the Best Looking Girl of Newcastle; local paper the *Evening Chronicle*'s 'Little Mr and Miss' competition; Mothercare's Happy Faces Portrait; and Most Attractive Girl in Gateshead's huge shopping complex the Metro Centre. Cheryl is a vegetarian and was the first girl to make it into Girls Aloud on *Popstars: The Rivals*.

★ ★ ★ ★ THE A–Z OF CELEBRITY TRIVIA ★ ★ ★ ★

★ Former *Dynasty* star **Joan Collins** posed semi-nude for *Playboy* magazine at the age of 50. Her first serious boyfriend after her husband Reed was Charlie Chaplin's son Sydney Chaplin. Collins left Chaplin for Arthur Loew Jr but the latter relationship ended in a bust-up at a New Year's bash. Loew famously called Collins 'a fucking bore' and Collins replied that Loew was 'a boring fuck'. Joan's father was once the agent of singer Don Arden, Sharon Osbourne's dad. Joan holds the *Guinness Book of Records* record for the world's largest unreturned payment for manuscript that was never published – 1.3 million dollars. Joan was amazed when a fan slid a piece of paper under a toilet door and asked for her autograph. She's never given an autograph since.

★ Drummer and singer-songwriter **Phil Collins** lost his virginity in an allotment. He was 14 years old.

★ *A Beautiful Mind* star **Jennifer Connelly**, wife to Paul Bettany, is fluent in Italian and French, and she once made a pop single in Japan, which she sang in phonetic Japanese.

★ Scottish Bond **Sean Connery** was a bricklayer, lifeguard and coffin polisher before he was famous. Sean spent much of his free time bodybuilding, a

★ ★ ★ ★ THE A-Z OF CELEBRITY TRIVIA ★ ★ ★ ★

pastime that eventually started his acting career. His hobby of bodybuilding culminated in a bid for the 1950 Mr Universe title. He came third. Sean has to have tattoos, which declare his love for his mum, his dad and his country, covered up by make-up when filming. When he was taking martial arts lessons from Steven Seagal for the James Bond film *Never Say Never Again*, Seagal broke Sean's wrist – allegedly because he cracked a joke about Seagal's mother.

★ TV funnyman turned Hollywood player **Steve Coogan** based his most famous character, Alan Partridge, on a radio presenter who interviewed him just as he was becoming famous.

★ Hip hop star **LL Cool J**'s name stands for Ladies Love Cool James. His real name is James Todd Smith III. As an actor he states his main influence as martial artist Bruce Lee.

★ Rock legend **Alice Cooper** is a born-again Christian.

★ Born Frank Cooper, **Gary Cooper**'s agent persuaded him to change to Gary after the agent's home town – Gary, Indiana.

★ ★ ★ ★ THE A-Z OF CELEBRITY TRIVIA ★ ★ ★ ★

★ **Andrea Corr** once received a request for an autograph while she was vomiting. The Corrs star told the fan to wait while she washed her hands.

★ The R Whites lemonade song 'I'm a secret lemonade drinker' was sung by **Elvis Costello**'s dad, Ross MacManus. Elvis provided the backing vocals.

★ A teenage **Kevin Costner** appeared in a soft-porn film about three young women and their love lives. *Sizzle Beach* was shot in 1974. The Hollywood star has been second choice to Harrison Ford for a role in two films: *JFK* and *Dragonfly*.

★ TV presenter **Fearne Cotton** loves peanut butter and she has two cats called Tallulah and Keloy.

★ **Simon Cowell** dropped out of school at the age of 16 and one of his first jobs was as a mail boy. In 2007, Simon was offered £1 million to become the face of Viagra. Insulted by the offer, he turned it down. Simon featured in *Scary Movie 3* where he played a judge of a rap contest. Simon once had wannabe pop stars on *American Idol* banned from singing 'Falling' by Alicia Keys because he was so tired of the song. His fellow judges Paula Abdul and Randy Jackson were in wholehearted agreement. His indulgences are houses and cars, of which he owns several, and the hard-working vegetarian takes just one holiday a year – usually to Barbados. Simon can't sing or play an instrument, doesn't know how to use an iPod and prefers watching TV to listening to CDs.

★ **Courtney Cox Arquette** was the first person to say 'period' on American TV in an advert for tampons. *Friends* star Courtney auditioned for the role of Princess Buttercup in *The Princess Bride*.

★ **Nadine Coyle** was the third girl to make it into Girls Aloud on *Popstars: The Rivals*. She has actually won two series of *Pop Stars*, the first was in Ireland where she was to become part of the group Six, but she was disqualified when the producers found out she was only 15. The minimum age of entry was 18. Pop impresario Louis Walsh has promised to make Nadine a solo star should Girls Aloud ever go their separate ways. Nadine supports Glasgow Celtic FC and her lucky numbers are five and nine.

★ Actor **Daniel Craig**'s middle name is Wroughton. Daniel is the first actor to play James Bond who was born after the Bond series began. He is Britain's highest-paid actor after signing a multi-million-dollar deal to continue playing 007. He will receive $10 million for his

★ ★ ★ ★ THE A-Z OF CELEBRITY TRIVIA ★ ★ ★ ★

return in *Quantum of Solace* and $16 million for Bond 23. A fan once took a picture of him using a urinal, which might explain his decision to grow a beard in a bid to stop being recognised by fans. He was voted the sexiest man alive in a poll by Durex in 2006.

★ Whenever Hollywood actress **Joan Crawford** changed a husband, she would have all of the toilet seats in the house changed.

★ *Phantom of the Opera* star **Michael Crawford** was once called Michael Dumble-Smith. The unsurprising desire for a name change was concluded after he saw a passing Crawford's biscuit lorry.

★ **Sheryl Crow**'s front two teeth are fake – the Grammy Award-winning singer had them knocked out when she tripped on the stage earlier in her career.

★ Gladiator **Russell Crowe** was once a pompadoured singer named Russ Le Roq. His first single was 'I want to be like Marlon Brando', even though he'd never seen a Brando movie when he wrote the song. Russell lost his front tooth playing rugby when he was ten. He didn't have it fixed until the director for *The Crossing* insisted. Russell paid for it out of his own pocket. Russell is now is in a band called 30 Odd Foot of

★ ★ ★ ★ THE A-Z OF CELEBRITY TRIVIA ★ ★ ★ ★

Grunts. They played their first US concert in Austin, Texas, in August 2000, following the success of *Gladiator*. Two of Russell's cousins are former New Zealand international cricketers.

★ Hollywood superstar **Tom Cruise** admits that he still does the *Risky Business* underwear dance when he's at home alone. He calls it his 'dance of freedom'. He was voted 'Least Likely to Succeed' at school. Tom once enrolled in a seminary to become a priest but dropped out after only one year.

★ 'Spanish enchantress' **Penelope Cruz** is a collector of coat hangers. She became a vegetarian in 2000 after filming *All the Pretty Horses*. She was the first Spanish actress ever to be nominated for an Oscar.

★ As a child Hollywood star **Billy Crystal** had a celebrity babysitter: legendary jazz singer Billie Holiday.

★ US rapper **Ice Cube** has six television screens in his SUV.

★ Everyone's favourite child actor **Macaulay Culkin** was arrested for possession of 17 grams of marijuana and prescription drug Xanax in 2004. He had to agree to drug counselling.

★ ★ ★ ★ THE A–Z OF CELEBRITY TRIVIA ★ ★ ★ ★

★ **Jamie Lee Curtis** says plastic surgery makes her look weird and claims it is the worst thing she's ever done. The US actress insured her legs for $2 million.

★ *24* star **Elisha Cuthbert** is a former foot model. For her 22nd birthday, she was given Paris Hilton's autobiography and perfume as a gift … *from* Paris Hilton. She was once a host on Canadian television show *Popular Mechanics for Kids*.

★ Welsh actor **Timothy Dalton** loves fishing, particularly in the Pacific Ocean. Dalton's Bond was the last of the Bonds to smoke cigarettes.

★ *Bourne* trilogy star **Matt Damon**'s middle name is Paige. Matt's grandfather is Finnish and he started a bowling league in Berlin while filming *The Bourne Supremacy*. He used to live with *Good Will Hunting* co-star Ben Affleck. As a teenager, Matt earned extra cash as a sidewalk break-dancer. Damon lost three-and-a-half stone to realistically play the role of a heroin addict in the 1996 movie *Courage Under Fire*. But the star admitted his strict exercise and diet regime was too dramatic. 'I went too far,' he said. 'I got sick and I wouldn't do that again because it was just too much.'

★ ★ ★ ★ THE A-Z OF CELEBRITY TRIVIA ★ ★ ★ ★

★ **Claire Danes** has a swing in her apartment. 'My parents had a swing, a trapeze and a trampoline in their apartment, I was inspired by that.' The star of *My So-called Life* and *Shopgirl* was banned from the Philippines in September 1998 for making derogatory remarks about the country. The President of the Philippines condemned her publicly.

★ Hip-hop mogul **Damon Dash** owns more than 3,000 pairs of trainers and never wears the same clothes twice. He refuses to write in red ink because he associates it with losing money.

★ *Pirates of the Caribbean* star **Jack Davenport**'s uncle is former Conservative MP Jonathan Aitken.

★ Pop star **Craig David** was suspended from the Football Association over an unpaid fee for the hire of football pitches for his Sunday-league team. Craig is a staunch supporter of Southampton FC and an only child.

★ *Curb Your Enthusiasm*'s **Larry David** is the co-creator of *Seinfeld*, and is estimated to have earned over $200 million from the show. He was considered for the part that went to Billy Bob Thornton in the film *Bad Santa*.

★ ★ ★ ★ THE A–Z OF CELEBRITY TRIVIA ★ ★ ★ ★

★ Comedian **Jim Davidson** married Alison Holloway after a three-week romance.

★ The purple *Big Brother* diary room chair was grabbed at auction by comedian **Alan Davies** in a head-to-head bidding war with Nasty Nick, whose final bid of £30,000 was topped by one penny by the comedian.

★ Screen legend **Bette Davis** started out as Ruth Davis but changed to Bette after Balzac's cousin Bette. Bette's waistline was insured for $28,000.

★ *Thelma & Louise* star **Geena Davis** tried to qualify for the US Olympic Archery Team in 1999.

★ **Kristin Davis**, who plays Charlotte in *Sex and the City*, got her big break when she landed a role in American TV drama *Melrose Place*. She left the show after one year when producers found that viewers disliked her character. She is the only of the four main actresses from *Sex and the City* to guest-star on *Friends*, and her favourite sweets are Peppermint Patties.

★ *The Office* star **Lucy Davis**'s father is comedian Jasper Carrott.

★ ★ ★ ★ THE A–Z OF CELEBRITY TRIVIA ★ ★ ★ ★

★ There's more to **Steve Davis** than just snooker. He loves a game of chess too.

★ Screen icon **James Dean** crashed and died in a Porsche Spydor.

★ **Cat Deeley** is known for hosting most of her shows barefoot. The TV presenter says she feels more comfortable and at home presenting this way. She hosted ITV's music show *CD:UK* longer than anyone else – from 1998 to 2005. Cat now lives in LA. She is partial to Ben and Jerry's ice cream.

★ Comedian and presenter **Ellen DeGeneres** turned down a role in *Friends* before signing up for a show called *These Friends of Mine* – the show was renamed *Ellen*. She used to be a vacuum cleaner saleswoman. At Walt Disney World's Epcot Park, there is an eco-themed ride named after her: Ellen's Energy World.

★ *Grey's Anatomy* star **Patrick Dempsey** began his career as a juggling unicycle-riding clown.

★ **Dame Judi Dench** won Best Supporting Actress in 1998 for *Shakespeare in Love*, despite only being onscreen for eight minutes, the shortest screen time ever for an Oscar winner. She is a collector of doll's

★ ★ ★ ★ THE A-Z OF CELEBRITY TRIVIA ★ ★ ★ ★

houses and furniture and was once invited to tell
stories on children's TV show *Rainbow.*

★ Proving that acting was always in his blood, **Robert
De Niro** appeared in his school play, *The Wizard of Oz*,
when he was ten years old. He played the Cowardly
Lion. Bob has an honorary doctorate from the
University of New York.

★ **Les Dennis** supports Liverpool FC. The comedian
also loves going power walking.

★ Hollywood heartthrob **Johnny Depp** suffers from
coulrophobia – fear of clowns. Johnny plays lead slide
guitar on the Oasis track 'Fade In-Out', from the band's
1997 album *Be Here Now.* Noel Gallagher was allegedly
too drunk to perform it himself. He wrote his own
theme music for his part in 2003's *Once Upon a Time in
Mexico.* He lost the role of Johnny Blaze in *Ghost Rider*
to Nicolas Cage and the role of Mr Smith in *Mr and
Mrs Smith* to Brad Pitt. When Johnny was engaged to
actress Winona Ryder, he had a tattoo saying 'Winona
forever' on his arm. After they separated, he had the 'n'
and 'a' removed to say 'Wino forever!'

★ American actress **Laura Dern** was constantly bullied
during her school years because her actor father, Bruce

★ ★ ★ ★ THE A–Z OF CELEBRITY TRIVIA ★ ★ ★ ★

Dern, was the only man ever to have killed Western actor John Wayne in a movie.

★ Celeb jockey **Frankie Dettori** once hosted *Top Of The Pops*, promotes his own range of foods and has received a police caution for possessing cocaine.

★ Model **Agyness Deyn**'s real name is Laura Hollins. Her first job was in a fish 'n' chip shop.

★ **Cameron Diaz** was nicknamed 'Skeletor' when she was at school because she was so skinny. *There's Something About Mary* star Cameron once won over £3,000 on the lottery. Several sources, including *Autograph Magazine*, have cited Cameron as one of the most difficult autograph-signers. On being asked to sign her name, she has been known to lecture fans about how silly autographs are. Cameron briefly dated pro-surfer Kelly Slater, and once broke her nose in a surfing accident. Cameron also likes to do her bit for the environment whenever she can. When she's being taken to award ceremonies in LA, she uses the Evo Limo Luxury Car Service – all of their vehicles run on natural gases. Her middle name is Michelle.

★ **Leonardo DiCaprio** was fired from his first job on the children's show *Romper Room* for being disruptive

★★★★ THE A-Z OF CELEBRITY TRIVIA ★★★★

– he was four at the time. At junior high school, Leo scared his teachers with his imitation of murderer Charles Manson. In 2005, the *Titanic* star snapped up a 104-acre island off the coast of Belize, and his favourite food is pasta. His middle name is Wilhelm.

★ Actress and singer **Angie Dickinson** insured her legs for $1 million.

★ *The Fast and the Furious* star **Vin Diesel** has a twin brother called Paul.

★ Iconic German actress and singer **Marlene Dietrich** was an insomniac.

★ Hollywood heartthrob **Matt Dillon**'s middle name is Raymond.

★ *Ground Force*'s **Charlie Dimmock** thought she was going to become a forensic scientist. She ended up famous as a TV gardener who didn't wear a bra.

★ When performing, **Celine Dion** requires a children's choir with 20 children of varying races. The Canadian balladeer is a big fan of television programme *Deal or No Deal* and has her own range of perfume.

★ ★ ★ ★ THE A-Z OF CELEBRITY TRIVIA ★ ★ ★ ★

★ **Walt Disney** died on 15 December 1966, yet a rumour has long existed that his body was cryogenically frozen and held under Disneyland's Pirates of the Caribbean ride. The origin of this urban legend is unknown.

★ **Beth Ditto** writes an advice column for British newspaper the *Guardian* called 'What Would Beth Ditto Do?' The Gossip singer does not shave her armpits or use deodorant.

★ Former Mis-teeq star and *Strictly Come Dancing* winner **Alesha Dixon** sold the wedding dress she wore when she married former So Solid Crew star Harvey on eBay for £7,500. She has one sister and five brothers.

★ Scouse comic **Ken Dodd**'s teeth are insured for $7.4 million.

★ Much of Babyshambles frontman **Pete Doherty**'s upbringing was spent in army garrisons where his father was an officer in the British Army. In his late teens he worked filling graves with soil. When he wasn't working, you could find Pete sitting on gravestones reading and writing. Tabloid favourite Doherty is a devoted Queens Park Rangers fan.

★ ★ ★ ★ THE A-Z OF CELEBRITY TRIVIA ★ ★ ★ ★

★ Hollywood legend and Catherine Zeta Jones's father-in-law **Kirk Douglas** has survived a helicopter crash. The helicopter collided with a stunt plane, killing two people aboard the plane.

★ *Romancing the Stone* co-stars **Michael Douglas** and **Danny DeVito** once shared a flat together.

★ **Robert Downey Jr** sang on the *Ally McBeal* Christmas CD during his stint on the show. The Hollywood bad boy dated *Sex and the City* star Sarah Jessica Parker during the 1980s.

★ British actress **Minnie Driver** is a keen surfer. Her boyfriend Matt Damon publicly dumped her on the *Oprah Winfrey Show*.

★ *X-Files* star **David Duchovny** damaged his eye playing basketball at school. He uses dye to maintain the right colour and stop the pupil from appearing too dilated.

★ While performing at one of her concerts, *Lizzie McGuire* star **Hilary Duff** chipped one of her front teeth on a microphone. She later got dental veneers. Hilary has her own celebrity Barbie doll named after her, and she's also designed clothes for Barbie. The Duff doll has a polka-dot dress with a red sash.

★ ★ ★ ★ THE A–Z OF CELEBRITY TRIVIA ★ ★ ★ ★

★ Singer **Duffy**'s early musical interest was inspired by her dad's videotape of the 1960s rock show *Ready Steady Go!* Duffy began singing at the age of six but was chucked out of her school choir for her voice. According to Duffy, 'It was too big and I didn't fit in.' Duffy earned 3 MOJO Award nominations in 2008 for *Album of the Year*, *Song of the Year* and *Breakthrough Act* – the most nominations for any one act.

★ US actress **Faye Dunaway** used to eat just one meal a day so that she could keep her slim figure.

★ *Spider-Man* actress **Kirsten Dunst** once appeared in a TV ad for a doll with all its bodily functions when she was a child. On the set of *ER*, George Clooney taught Kirsten to drive using his studio golf cart. Caroline is her middle name.

★ **Duran Duran** got their name from an astronaut in the Jane Fonda film *Barbarella*.

★ 60s icon **Bob Dylan** appeared in the 1973 film *Pat Garrett and Billy the Kid* as a character called Alias.

★ *Deal or No Deal* presenter **Noel Edmonds** is an only child.

★ ★ ★ ★ THE A-Z OF CELEBRITY TRIVIA ★ ★ ★ ★

★ Swedish actress **Britt Ekland** sang backing vocals on Rod Stewart's song 'Tonight's The Night'.

★ Former *Baywatch* star **Carmen Electra** is unable to swim and admits she hates water. Pop legend Prince was responsible for giving her her stage name.

★ **Eminem**'s two favourite places to play on tour are Amsterdam – for the liberal laws – and London for its food. The rapper's parents fronted a covers group called Daddy Warbucks. His favourite film is *Scarface* and his favourite flavour of ice cream is cookie dough.

★ Comedian **Harry Enfield** is an only child.

★ Brat Pack actor **Emilio Estevez** is Martin Sheen's eldest son. His father decided to use the stage name 'Sheen' over his more ethnic-sounding birth name 'Estevez', and Emilio chose to retain the family name, hoping to avoid accusations of profiting from his father's name. He also thought the double 'E' set of initials was 'pretty'. Emilio was once engaged to Demi Moore. He lost the lead role in *Gremlins* to Zach Galigan.

★ Eccentric boxer **Chris Eubank** holds an HGV licence. He failed his test three times before finally passing, thus enabling himself to drive his private truck.

★ ★ ★ ★ THE A-Z OF CELEBRITY TRIVIA ★ ★ ★ ★

★ Radio 2 DJ and reformed wildman **Chris Evans** was born on April Fool's Day. For a man who left school at 16 and had over 20 jobs in less than four years, including a stint as a Tarzanogram, Evans built an incredible career for himself. In 2000, he sold Ginger Media Group, the company he founded, for £225 million, pocketing £75 million. He has a pilot licence and owns a helicopter. He had a stall on Camden market in 2004 where he used to sell some of his possessions.

★ Funnyman **Lee Evans** is not very fond of the colour green. In fact, he is scared of it and once panicked when forced to wear a green suit.

★ Television presenter **Jenni Falconer** went to Leeds University in 1994, but she dropped out. She did achieve something of note during her time there: she appeared on *Blind Date*.

★ Actor **Peter Falk**, best known for his role as TV detective Columbo, has a glass eye.

★ Irish bad boy **Colin Farrell** likes to check into hotels under the moniker Tom Foolery. Colin's middle name is James, but using this would clearly spoil his tomfoolery. He has suffered from chronic insomnia

★ ★ ★ ★ THE A-Z OF CELEBRITY TRIVIA ★ ★ ★ ★

since he was 12 years old and he once auditioned to become a member of Boyzone. His dad Eamon was an Irish footballer. Fans of television programme *Ballykissangel* remember Colin fondly. Colin says that Marilyn Monroe was the first woman he fell in love with. 'I used to leave Smarties, the Irish equivalent of M&Ms, under my pillow with a little note saying, "I know you're dead but these are very tasty and you should come and have a few. I won't tell anyone".' Colin is now trilingual. He can speak German, French and English, and he suffers from a fear of flying.

★ US actress and humanitarian campaigner **Mia Farrow**, former partner of director Woody Allen, once quipped that her vital statistics were 20–20–20.

★ Former footballer and *I'm a Celebrity … Get Me Out of Here!* contestant **John Fashanu** is a black belt in karate.

★ Former *Spooks* and *Holby City* actress **Lisa Faulkner** once auditioned for a role in James Bond film *Die Another Day*, but admitted it went terribly. Halle Berry eventually landed the role.

★ Charlie's Angel **Farrah Fawcett** was once afforded the honour of having a gold-plated bathroom tap named after her: the Farrah Faucet.

★★★★ THE A-Z OF CELEBRITY TRIVIA ★★★★

★ Ex-husband of Britney Spears **Kevin Federline** was voted 'Most Likely to Be on *America's Most Wanted*' at school. Kevin has worked as a dancer for Pink and Michael Jackson. Since his split with Britney, Kevin has been nicknamed 'Fed-Ex'.

★ Broadcaster and TV host **Vanessa Feltz** revealed that her first snog was with DJ Pete Tong. She has a first-class degree in English from Cambridge.

★ *Ugly Betty* star **America Ferrera** insured her smile for $10 million.

★ **Noel Fielding** has a sweet tooth, yet the star of *The Mighty Boosh* can't eat chocolate because of liver problems. He is good pals with fellow comedian Russell Brand.

★ TV presenter **Judy Finnegan** had elocution lessons to hide her Mancunian accent. When accepting an award with husband Richard Madeley at the National Television Awards in October 2000, Judy's dress famously fell open to reveal her cleavage.

★ *Star Wars* actress **Carrie Fisher** had to stand on a box to reach Harrison Ford during their kissing scenes. She regularly works as a script doctor in Hollywood and was once engaged to actor Dan Aykroyd.

★★★★ THE A–Z OF CELEBRITY TRIVIA ★★★★

★ 'Lord of the Dance' **Michael Flatley**'s legs are insured for £25 million.

★ *Ally McBeal* star **Calista Flockhart**'s dog was her best friend until he died.

★ Hollywood legend **Jane Fonda** has been a Christian since 2001.

★ **Harrison Ford** drinks out of a cup decorated with his and partner Calista Flockhart's pictures and names. The *Indiana Jones* star was bullied by his classmates at school because he liked to hang out with girls. The scar on his face is from a car accident. He has admitted to suffering from OCD (Obsessive-Compulsive Disorder). Harrison lost the part of Sam Bowden in *Cape Fear* to Nick Nolte. He was also considered for the role of Sam in *Ghost* and for Tom Hanks' Academy Award–nominated role in *Saving Private Ryan*. Two of his films, *Raiders of the Lost Ark* and *Star Wars*, have spawned Disneyland rides. Until 1970 he was billed as Harrison J Ford to prevent confusion with silent-screen actor Harrison Ford. He actually has no middle name

In 1993, the aracnologist Norman Platnick named a new species of spider *Calponia Harrisonfordi* and, in 2002, an entomologist named a new ant species *Pheidole Harrisonfordi* in recognition of Harrison's work as Vice Chairman of Conservation International.

★ Veteran presenter and national institution **Bruce Forsyth** was on television for the first time in 1938. He is a proud supporter of Tottenham Hotspur FC and has been married three times, including to his current wife, former Miss World Winelia Merced, since 1979. He has five daughters and one son and is a great-grandfather. He is believed to be responsible for more catchphrases than any other presenter in the history of British television.

★ **Jodie Foster** was George Lucas's second choice to play Princess Leia in *Star Wars*. Foster had to undergo psychiatric evaluation when she was 13 years old before taking on the role of a teenage prostitute in the 1976 film *Taxi Driver*. This was to make sure that she would be capable of handling a potentially traumatic role. Jodie's first role was in a Coppertone advert at the age of three. The advert also featured a dog, which pulled her pants down. Jodie still found time to go to Yale University when she grew up. Jodie got the lead role in *The Silence of the Lambs* after Michelle Pfeiffer turned it down.

★ ★ ★ ★ THE A-Z OF CELEBRITY TRIVIA ★ ★ ★ ★

★ Former Page 3 girl **Sam Fox** once starred in a Bollywood film and fronted her own strip poker computer game – Samantha Fox Strip Poker – in the 1980s.

★ **Vivica A Fox**, star of *Kill Bill*, ruined a $1.5 million diamond-encrusted dress when she spilled red wine over it at an Oscar party.

★ As a second grader, Oscar-winning *Ray* star **Jamie Foxx** was so talented at telling jokes his teacher used him as a reward. If the class behaved, Jamie would entertain them.

★ It must have been destiny: former Destiny's Child singer **Farrah Franklin**'s middle name is Destiny.

★ *Shawshank Redemption* star **Morgan Freeman** is a trained ballet dancer.

★ **Dawn French** was voted the number-one female role model in the UK in a survey of 1,000 schoolgirls in 2004. The comedienne once appeared with John Cleese in a business training video called *The Balance Sheet Barrier*.

★ Presenter **Mariella Frostrup** had a relationship with Hollywood heartthrob George Clooney in the 80s.

★ ★ ★ ★ THE A-Z OF CELEBRITY TRIVIA ★ ★ ★ ★

★ TV presenter and writer **Stephen Fry** had gained nine O levels by the age of 13. When he was 18, he was jailed for credit card fraud.

★ Hollywood legend **Clark Gable** was listed on his birth certificate as a girl.

★ **Zsa Zsa Gabor** wins the list of most married female celebrities with a record nine husbands. The flamboyant actress is also Paris Hilton's great-aunt.

★ When television presenter **Kirsty Gallacher** was a child, she accidentally whacked professional golfer Nick Faldo with a golf club when she was swinging for the ball. He still has the scar.

★ Oasis star **Liam Gallagher** once won the top prize in *Nuts* magazine's prestigious 'man boobs' awards. Liam's childhood nickname was Weetabix, because he was always scoffing the cereal, and his favourite films are *Quadrophenia*, *Trainspotting*, *Seven* and *Scarface*.

★ **Noel Gallagher** was a roadie for the Inspiral Carpets before he shot to stardom in band Oasis. He was nicknamed Brezhnev at school.

★ *Ocean's Eleven* actor **Andy Garcia** was a Siamese twin.

★ ★ ★ ★ THE A-Z OF CELEBRITY TRIVIA ★ ★ ★ ★

★ Hollywood icon **Judy Garland** was afraid of horses. In 1979, her false eyelashes were auctioned off for $125.

★ **Jennifer Garner,** who is married to Ben Affleck, almost got arrested the day of her prom. The *Elektra* star and a friend were sunbathing topless in a park when police spotted them.

★ *Pop Idol* runner-up **Gareth Gates** supports Leeds United FC and has cured his stammer.

★ **Bob Geldof** did not excel as a child, and made up his own school reports to appease his father. Initially called the Nightlife Thugs, his band changed their name to the Boomtown Rats, after a gang in a Woody Guthrie song

★ Socialite and daughter of Bob **Peaches Geldof** has a tattoo on her ankle and another on her wrist. She is a vegetarian.

★ **Sarah Michelle Gellar**, aka Buffy The Vampire Slayer, became best friends with *Sabrina: The Teenage Witch* star Melissa Joan Hart while at acting school with her. Sarah is afraid of cemeteries, and was discovered by an agent while eating in a restaurant at the age of four. Sarah once appeared in a TV ad for Burger King when

★ ★ ★ ★ THE A-Z OF CELEBRITY TRIVIA ★ ★ ★ ★

she was a child. She had such a bad time saying the word 'Burger' that she needed a voice coach. It was the first American commercial ever to name a competitor; McDonalds subsequently sued both Sarah and Burger King. She was also a figure skater for three years and was ranked third in New York State.

★ **Richard Gere**'s middle name is Tiffany. The actor attended the University of Massachusetts on a scholarship for gymnastics. In the early 70s, Gere played Danny Zuko in a London production of *Grease*. He was once lead singer in a band called The Strangers.

★ Hollywood star **Gina Gershon** writes children's books with her brother Paul.

★ **Ricky Gervais**'s cat, Ollie, was given to him by television presenter and friend Jonathan Ross. Comedian and writer Ricky turned down £2 million to do an advert for an American drink company. 'I do things that I want to be proud of,' he said, 'so if I turn something down it's because I don't want to do it, not because the money isn't right.' He used to sing in a band called Seona Dancing.

★ **Mel Gibson** broke the school record for the most strappings in a week – 27. The *Braveheart* star

★ ★ ★ ★ THE A-Z OF CELEBRITY TRIVIA ★ ★ ★ ★

auditioned to play Mozart in *Amadeus* but lost the part to Tom Hulce. He also lost out to Robin Williams in *The Dead Poet's Society*.

★ **Girls Aloud**, who originated from talent show *Popstars: The Rivals*, hold the record for the shortest time elapsed from formation to reaching UK number one. The *Observer* labelled 'Biology' as the single of the decade. In 2007, the band signed a deal thought to be worth £1.25 million to endorse Sunsilk haircare products.

★ When performing comedy, **Whoopi Goldberg**'s original stage name was Whoopee Cushion. Whoopi's real name is Caryn Johnson. She worked as a bricklayer, bank teller and a makeup artist in a funeral parlour before becoming famous.

★ **DJ Goldie**'s nickname didn't result from his gold teeth, but from the golden dreadlocks he once sported. His real name is Clifford Price.

★ Motor-mouthed Hollywood star **Cuba Gooding Jr** was once a backup dancer for Paula Abdul and he break-danced at the closing ceremony of the 1984 Olympic Games in Los Angeles. His acceptance speech at the 1997 Academy Awards topped the list of VH1's *20 Greatest Oscar Moments*.

★ ★ ★ ★ THE A-Z OF CELEBRITY TRIVIA ★ ★ ★ ★

★ Disgraced *Big Brother* contestant **Jade Goody** appeared in television show *London's Burning* at the age of five. Celebrity bible *Heat* sold more Jade Goody cover issues than those with Victoria Beckham on the front. Her own brand of perfume is called 'Ssh...' and Living TV made a show about making it called *Just Jade*. The first celebrities Jade met after her exit from the *Big Brother* house were Davina McCall, Leigh Francis, Graham Norton and Duncan from boy band Blue. Jade actually came fourth in *Big Brother 3*. When she was pregnant, Jade Goody developed a liking for pickled-onion-flavoured Monster Munch with hummus.

★ *Frasier* star **Kelsey Grammer** sings and plays the piano on the theme tune for the show

★ **Hugh Grant** has been an actor for around 20 years but claims he just fell into acting rather than it having been a true calling. Grant's films have earned over $2.4 billion. Quintessentially English Hugh is a descendant of former British Prime Minister Spencer Perceval. Among his many jobs he has worked as an assistant groundsman at Fulham FC and as an advertising executive.

★ *Withnail and I* star **Richard E Grant** is allergic to alcohol and doesn't smoke.

★★★★ THE A–Z OF CELEBRITY TRIVIA ★★★★

★ Acting couple **Melanie Griffith** and Don Johnson divorced and then tied the knot again.

★ *The Simpsons* creator **Matt Groening** managed to incorporate his own initials into the animated Homer. M is his hair and G is his ear. He plays in a band called Rock Bottom Remainders with horror novelist Stephen King.

★ **Jake Gyllenhaal** got his first driving lesson from family friend Paul Newman. The *Brokeback Mountain* star is a Buddhist and his favourite colour is green. His middle name is Benjamin.

★ **Maggie Gyllenhaal**'s father's family grew up with the Swedenborgian religion, and the American actress descends from the Swedish noble family of the same name. Maggie raises money for Trickle Up, a charity helping people combat poverty. She helped design a necklace that retails at $100 and raises money for the charity.

★ After doing her A-Levels, Ginger Spice **Geri Halliwell** travelled around Europe, picking up jobs here and there. She was a podium dancer in Majorca, a TV hostess in Turkey, and did a stint as a topless model. She also took on more mundane jobs such as aerobics teacher and barmaid.

★ ★ ★ ★ THE A-Z OF CELEBRITY TRIVIA ★ ★ ★ ★

★ 'U Can't Touch This' star **MC Hammer** was declared bankrupt in 1996, with debts of over $10 million, despite his wealth at one time being estimated at $20 million.

★ **Tom Hanks** is a distant relation of an ex-US president. The Oscar-nominated *Saving Private Ryan* star is a third cousin four times removed to Abraham Lincoln, the 16th President of the United States. Tom gave *Road to Perdition* co-star Tyler Hoechlin – Hanks played his father in the film – $16 for his 16th birthday present.

★ **Daryl Hannah** was so shy as a child that at one point she was diagnosed as borderline autistic. Even today the *Kill Bill* actress says she likes to just sit in a corner and observe people. Her brother Don is a skydiving instructor.

★ Girls Aloud star **Sarah Harding** once entered *FHM* magazine's national beauty contest 'High Street Honeys' and her pictures appeared in the first Top 100. But she withdrew when success on *Popstars: The Rivals* came calling. Sarah signed a £100,000 deal to model for Ultimo lingerie, following in the footsteps of models Penny Lancaster and Rachel Hunter. She was the last girl to make it into Girls Aloud on

★ ★ ★ ★ THE A-Z OF CELEBRITY TRIVIA ★ ★ ★ ★

Popstars: The Rivals. She also dated on of the boys – Mikey Green – in the rival group Phixx. Sarah's middle name is Nicole and the first concert she ever went to see was Eminem.

★ *Cheers'* **Woody Harrelson** was once arrested for planting four marijuana hemp seeds in rural Kentucky. The actor was challenging a law that failed to distinguish between marijuana and hemp. All charges against him were dismissed. Woody's father has served time in prison for murder.

★ TV chef and presenter **Ainsley Harriott** used to be a ball-boy at Wimbledon.

★ Esteemed actor **Richard Harris** was seen wearing an elastoplast on his neck when playing King Arthur in the film *Camelot*.

★ TV presenter and artist **Rolf Harris** was Australia's Junior Backstroke Champion in 1946.

★ Beatle **George Harrison** was arrested along with his soon-to-be wife on his wedding day in 1969. The charges? Marijuana possession.

★ ★ ★ ★ THE A-Z OF CELEBRITY TRIVIA ★ ★ ★ ★

★ Heartthrob actor **Josh Hartnett** auditioned six times for *Dawson's Creek*, but wasn't given a part in the show. He used to be a vegetarian and his middle name is Daniel.

★ **David Hasselhoff**'s great-uncle, Karl Hasselhoff, invented the inflatable sheep. 'The Hoff', as he is affectionately known, has only ever had one number-one song in the German pop charts – 1989's 'Looking for Freedom'. Something of an Internet phenomenon, his fans have supported the website 'Get Hasselhoff to Number One' in a bid to get one of his singles to the top of the charts. He is a veritable tower of a man at 6 feet four inches tall.

★ In 1985, Desperate Housewife **Teri Hatcher** played a dancing mermaid on *The Love Boat*. 'That was the first job I ever had,' she says. 'I left college before finishing my math degree to go do that.'

★ *Becoming Jane* and *The Princess Diaries* star **Anne Hathaway** trained extensively as a soprano and performed as a member of the All-Eastern United States High School Honors Chorus at New York City's Carnegie Hall in 1999. Anne is lactose intolerant, has a dog named Esmerelda and she cites reading and interior design as her hobbies.

★ ★ ★ ★ THE A-Z OF CELEBRITY TRIVIA ★ ★ ★ ★

★ Actress **Goldie Hawn** was a professional dancer and appeared as a go-go dancer in New York City before she was famous.

★ Mexican actress **Salma Hayek** was expelled from school for setting all the clocks back three hours.

★ *Big Brother* star **Chanelle Hayes** cites her best experience since leaving the house as meeting Victoria Beckham at her book signing. Chanelle walked out of the *Big Brother* house on day 62.

★ *Playboy* boss **Hugh Hefner** celebrated the magazine's 50th anniversary in style. He auctioned off his address book, which contained the numbers of some of the most glamorous women in the world, alongside portraits of the likes of Brigitte Bardot.

★ *Grey's Anatomy* blonde bombshell **Katherine Heigl** starred in the lowest-earning movie in recorded history, 2006 thriller *Zyzzyx Road* with Tom Sizemore. It grossed $30 at the box office. Katherine's favourite movie is *The 40 Year Old Virgin*, which she watches over and over again.

★ Music icons **Jimi Hendrix**, **Janis Joplin** and **Jim Morrison** were all 27 years old when they died.

★ ★ ★ ★ THE A–Z OF CELEBRITY TRIVIA ★ ★ ★ ★

★ For a couple of weeks during 2003, comedian **Lenny Henry** voiced the speaking clock for BT as part of Comic Relief. Even he struggled to make the time funny.

★ *Breakfast at Tiffany's* star **Audrey Hepburn** was in Nazi-occupied Holland during World War II and almost starved to death. She lived on two loaves of bread for an entire month.

★ Only one woman has ever won four Oscars for Best Actress: **Katharine Hepburn**. Screen legend Katharine had such a phobia of dirty hair that when she was on the set she would sniff everybody's hair to make sure that it had been washed. As a child, she would shave her head, wear trousers and call herself Jimmy because she wanted to be a boy.

★ **Victoria Hervey** is the daughter of Victor, the sixth Marquess of Bristol, who was the first member of his family to go to prison for theft. Lady V once dated Danish restaurateur Mogens Tholstrup. Mogens was 15 years her senior, and she used to call him 'Grandpa'. Victoria has confessed that her ideal man is 'probably gay'.

★ Hollywood star **Jennifer Love Hewitt** regularly checks into hotels under the name Winnie the Pooh.

★ ★ ★ ★ THE A-Z OF CELEBRITY TRIVIA ★ ★ ★ ★

★ Before he was a racing driving, **Damon Hill** was the guitarist in a band called Sex Hitler and The Hormones.

★ Funnyman **Harry Hill**'s favourite television soap is *EastEnders*. He can sing 'How Much Is That Doggie In The Window' backwards. Until Ricky Gervais stole his crown, he had racked up the most appearances on *The Late Show With David Letterman* by a British comedian with seven.

★ **Paris Hilton** has trademarked her famous quip 'That's hot!' She has size-11 feet and once said, 'All those super cute shoes like Guccis and Manolos look like clown shoes on me.' In May 2007, after numerous scrapes with the law over driving incidents, Paris was sentenced to 45 days in a detention centre. She began her term in June but was released after just 22 days because of her good behaviour. Paris said she was a changed woman. Paris's mum Kathy Richards Hilton went to school with Janet Jackson. When her parents die, Paris, like her sister Nicky, expects to inherit over $15 million.

★ Legendary filmmaker **Alfred Hitchcock** never won an Oscar for directing. He did, however, direct *Blackmail* in 1931 – the first ever talking film made in England.

★ ★ ★ ★ THE A-Z OF CELEBRITY TRIVIA ★ ★ ★ ★

★ **Adolf Hitler**'s favourite movie was *King Kong*.

★ While filming *Finding Neverland*, actor **Dustin Hoffman** lost the tip of one finger and performed one day of filming while on morphine. Dustin began training to be a doctor, but never completed the course. He once said that one of the main reasons he went to acting school was for the girls.

★ *Britain's Got Talent* judge **Amanda Holden** supports PETA (People for the Ethical Treatment of Animals) in their campaign for a bearskin ban. She also supports Everton FC.

★ **Katie Holmes** turned down a place at Columbia University so she could play Joey Potter in *Dawson's Creek*. Katie is married to Tom Cruise and she was born two months premature, weighing in at only four pounds. Her favourite directors are Woody Allen, Ron Howard and Oliver Stone, and she loves diet coke and vanilla lattes.

★ While at school, Welsh actor **Anthony Hopkins** had a talent for drinking India ink, which impressed his school chums but not his teachers.

★ Gruff-voiced English actor **Bob Hoskins** is an only child. He was once a bouncer.

★ ★ ★ ★ THE A-Z OF CELEBRITY TRIVIA ★ ★ ★ ★

★ **Chantelle Houghton**, who won *Celebrity Big Brother* despite not being a celebrity, is scared of snakes and spiders. Her hair is naturally brown, and she describes herself as a 'bright, blonde bimbo'. Her favourite book is *Learning to Fly*, by Victoria Beckham. The book is about Victoria's rise to fame, not aviation.

★ Early in her career, **Whitney Houston** sang the jingle used in commercials for Bounce fabric sheets. She rides a Harley Davidson. The singer and actress was considered for the lead role in *What's Love Got to Do with It*.

★ Actress **Kate Hudson** doesn't like to watch herself on screen; she actually breaks into a cold sweat, and shakes when watching a performance. She is Goldie Hawn's daughter and her middle name is Garry. Kate buys her clothes from vintage clothing shops and makes her own jewellery. She doesn't like wearing makeup and is scared of mirrors. When actress Christina Ricci and Kate filmed 1999's *Desert Blue* together in a small Nevada town, the budding actresses lived in a motel dining on Spaghetti O's and Kraft Macaroni & Cheese.

★ Roy Scherer became **Rock Hudson** after his agent searched the globe for an alternative, coming up with

★ ★ ★ ★ THE A-Z OF CELEBRITY TRIVIA ★ ★ ★ ★

an amalgamation of the Hudson River and the Rock of Gibraltar.

★ Actress **Liz Hurley** was once recruited by famous London nightspot Annabel's to encourage younger members to join. In her teens, the model-to-be dyed her hair pink and pierced her nose. Lovely Liz scored a modelling contract after winning *Face of the Year* competition at a local newspaper in Winchester and went on to assist cricketer Imran Khan raise money for his cancer hospital in Pakistan. The *Austin Powers* star is godmother to Lennon Francis Gallagher, the son of Patsy Kensit. She once went for an audition to try out for Cassandra's character in *Only Fools and Horses.*

★ Generation X singer **Billy Idol** was strongly considered to play Jim Morrison in *The Doors.*

★ Actor **Rhys Ifans**'s first language is Welsh, and at one time he went to the all Welsh-speaking school Maes Garmon. He was the original lead singer for the band Super Furry Animals, but he left before the band became well known.

★ Spanish crooner **Julio Iglesias** used to be goalie for Real Madrid's youth team. He once had five gallons of water flown from Miami to LA so he could wash his hair.

★ ★ ★ ★ THE A-Z OF CELEBRITY TRIVIA ★ ★ ★ ★

★ Before he was famous, *Brideshead Revisited* actor **Jeremy Irons** had his sights set on becoming a vet.

★ The late Crocodile Hunter **Steve Irwin** got a pet Python for his sixth birthday. A portrait of him can be seen in the National Portrait Gallery in Australia, where his picture replaced that of Germaine Greer.

★ Musician and actor **Chris Isaak** used to work in a funeral parlour as an assistant.

★ Comedian **Eddie Izzard** sold out his 'Sexie' show in New York without any advertising or publicity. There was a time when he thought he was going to be an accountant.

★ **Hugh Jackman** spurned the opportunity to be the next Jason Donovan when he turned down a part in *Neighbours* early in his career. Hollywood heartthrob Hugh's first job was as a petrol station attendant on the midnight to dawn shift. He has appeared in four films with Halle Berry and sushi is his favourite food. He lost the role of Robert Langdon in *The Da Vinci Code* to Tom Hanks.

★ **Janet Jackson**'s 'wardrobe malfunction' at the 2004 Super Bowl, in which her bare breast was exposed by

★ ★ ★ ★ THE A-Z OF CELEBRITY TRIVIA ★ ★ ★ ★

Justin Timberlake, resulted in a $500,000 fine levied by the Federal Communications Commission to CBS. The 'Nipplegate' costs could be met using only 7.5 seconds of commercial time revenue from the Super Bowl telecast. Her boob flash is the most searched event in the history of the internet. Janet collects porcelain pigs.

★ 'Billie Jean' by **Michael Jackson** was the first video by a black artist to air on MTV. The pop legend once hired two private jets – one for him to travel in and one as a decoy to confuse the press – to travel from Nevada to California, at a combined cost of £14,705. He was made an honorary director of Exeter City FC, by his friend and co-director the spoon-bender Uri Geller. He owns the rights to the South Carolina State anthem.

★ Super-cool actor **Samuel L Jackson** got his part in the *Star Wars* film *The Phantom Menace* when he declared his love of the films on Chris Evans's show *TFI Friday* and director George Lucas was watching. Jackson was once a doorman at the Manhattan Plaza in New York. He was Bill Cosby's stand-in on *The Cosby Show* for two years.

★ **Mick Jagger** was a porter in a psychiatric hospital before he formed the Rolling Stones. He was also a

★ ★ ★ ★ **THE A-Z OF CELEBRITY TRIVIA** ★ ★ ★ ★

student at the London School of Economics. The veteran rocker turned down £3.5 million to write his memoirs, claiming he simply couldn't remember enough details from his own life.

★ 'Superstar' singer **Jamelia** won a record-breaking three MOBO Awards in 2003.

★ Australian broadcaster and journalist **Clive James** used to work as a lion-cage cleaner.

★ **Sir David Jason**, aka Del Boy, was a keen gymnast at school, and won awards for his skills. Sir David was born David White but, on discovering there was already an actor called David White, he renamed himself Jason after his younger brother, who died in infancy. He once had a small role on now-defunct soap *Crossroads*.

★ Hip-hop mogul **Jay-Z** was friends with the Notorious B.I.G. at school. His 2004 request to be knighted was refused by Prince Charles.

★ Rapper **Wyclef Jean**'s favourite pseudonym when checking into hotels is Dracula. He was born on the same day in the same year as Eminem – 17 October 1972.

★ ★ ★ ★ THE A-Z OF CELEBRITY TRIVIA ★ ★ ★ ★

★ American singer-songwriter **Billy Joel** was once a successful boxer, winning 22 out of his 24 fights. He quit when he broke his nose.

★ Screen siren **Scarlett Johanssen** was rejected by New York University's School of the Arts for 2003. She celebrated her 20th birthday at Disneyland. Scarlett has a twin brother, Hunter Johansson, who is three minutes younger than her. The Hollywood beauty likes to jest that those three minutes are the most important in her life.

★ **Elton John**'s first job earned him 50p a night. He was a piano player in a Middlesex pub. When performing, he demands that his dressing room be kept at 60°F in summer and 70°F in winter. Sir Elton won't play white pianos as he thinks they're tasteless. The same applies to a host of other things, including white limousines, but he can endure white refrigerators. His real name is Reginald Dwight, and he got the 'Elton' from sax player Elton Dean and the 'John' from Blues Inc founder Long John Baldry.

★ When she was just 14, **Angelina Jolie** dropped out of acting classes because she wanted to become a funeral director. Jolie has 13 known tattoos on her body. Among them is the Tennessee Williams quote 'A prayer

★ ★ ★ ★ THE A-Z OF CELEBRITY TRIVIA ★ ★ ★ ★

for the wild at heart, kept in cages' and four sets of geographical coordinates on her upper left arm which indicate of the birthplaces of her children. Jolie's uncle, Chip Taylor (who looks just like her father Jon Voight), wrote the song 'Wild Thing'. Ange's first baby with Brad Pitt will have a Namibian passport. The total rights to photographs of images of the baby earned approximately $10 million, all of which was donated to charity by the couple. There is even a waxwork figure of the baby in the New York Madame Tussaud's.

★ Comedian **Dom Joly** worked as a diplomat for the European Commission before going on to make *Trigger Happy TV*.

★ American musician **Norah Jones**'s father is the sitar virtuoso Ravi Shanker, but Norah was raised exclusively by her mother, receiving little contact with her dad or her Indian roots.

★ Welsh *T4* presenter **Steve Jones** was once described by his co-host June Sarpong as a 'serial snogger'. He used to be a model for Versace.

★ Singing legend **Tom Jones**'s real name is Thomas Woodward Junior, and he was the son of a coal miner. When the Welsh belter played Las Vegas in the 70s,

★ ★ ★ ★ THE A-Z OF CELEBRITY TRIVIA ★ ★ ★ ★

women used to throw their knickers and their keys on stage, and it was in Vegas that he met his good friend Elvis Presley. Tom married his wife when he was just 16 years old and they have stayed together for over 50 years. Before he was famous he spent a short time working as a vacuum salesman. He is now estimated to be worth £175 million, and his chest hair is insured for $7 million.

★ Man in Black **Tommy Lee Jones** was a roommate with former Vice President turned environmental champion Al Gore. He is a keen polo player.

★ Former weathergirl and Swedish tabloid favourite **Ulrika Jonsson** has a devil tattooed on her bottom.

★ Queen of celebs **Jordan** aka Katie Price has an older brother called Daniel and a younger sister called Sophie. She can speak Greek. She once ran as a candidate in the Stretford and Urmston election, promising a 'Bigger and Betta Future', free breast implants, a ban on parking tickets and an increase in nudist beaches. Her campaign was only to bring a little fun to a dull election, but she still received 713 votes – 1.8% of the votes cast. Katie once auditioned for a part on *Baywatch*.

★ ★ ★ ★ THE A-Z OF CELEBRITY TRIVIA ★ ★ ★ ★

★ **Milla Jovovich** performed all of her own stunts in *Resident Evil*. Her middle name is Natasha and her favourite TV shows are *The Simpsons*, *King of the Hill* and *Malcolm in the Middle*. She was once in a band called Plastic Has Memory.

★ Radio 1 DJ **Judge Jules**'s uncle is celebrity chef Rick Stein.

★ Comedian **Phill Jupitus** used to be a performance poet. He called himself 'Porky the Poet'.

★ Million-pound newsreader **Natasha Kaplinsky** used to get up at 3.20am every morning when she presented the BBC's *Breakfast*. She won the first series of *Strictly Come Dancing* with dance partner and eventually boyfriend Brendan Cole. During the training period for the show, Natasha put in 180 hours of dancing and she was the first ever contestant to earn a perfect ten from the judges. The hardest person she has ever had to interview was her own father – opening one question by addressing him as 'Dad' on air.

★ Former Atomic Kitten and face of Iceland supermarket **Kerry Katona** has published a novel called *Tough Love*. She left school at the age of 16 to become a stripper and has admitted to never singing on any of

★ ★ ★ ★ THE A-Z OF CELEBRITY TRIVIA ★ ★ ★ ★

Atomic Kitten's songs. She has been voted Celebrity Mum of the Year twice, and the Worst Celebrity Mum of the Year once.

★ TV presenter **Vernon Kay** worked as a cleaner until he was spotted by a modelling agency. He became a model before moving on to TV work. Throughout his life, he has supported Bolton Wanderers FC.

★ **Ronan Keating** was once named Spectacle Wearer of the Year, yet he doesn't even wear glasses! The singer once had to abandon a film shoot when he was flashed at by streakers in Phuket, Thailand.

★ *Reservoir Dogs'* Mr White **Harvey Keitel** used to have a stammer.

★ **Grace Kelly**, aka Princess Grace of Monaco, was the first actress to appear on a postage stamp.

★ When popular Scottish presenter **Lorraine Kell**y started out in broadcasting she was told to take elocution lessons if she wanted to get anywhere.

★ Manchester-born **Matthew Kelly**'s first job after leaving school was as a bingo caller. Before going on to present *Stars In Their Eyes*, he was a Shakespearean actor.

★ ★ ★ ★ THE A–Z OF CELEBRITY TRIVIA ★ ★ ★ ★

★ R&B star **R Kelly** wrote Michael Jackson's song 'You Are Not Alone' and he likes to wear French braids.

★ Singer and actor **Martin Kemp** wed his long-time girlfriend Shirlie, a former Wham! backing singer. The couple met through George Michael, and Shirlie still runs his fanclub.

★ Before acting in *EastEnders*, **Ross Kemp** was a singer in a Fruit and Fibre advert for Kellogg's. As the candidate of the Glasgow University Labour Club, Kemp was elected Rector. His mum was a hairdresser, and his dad was a policeman. He supports West Ham United FC.

★ *The Good Life* star **Felicity Kendal** was nicknamed 'Fatty Foo' when she was at school.

★ In 1985, a four-year-old **Alicia Keys** appeared on *The Cosby Show* as one of the guests at Rudy's slumber party. While on the road, Alicia carries 'a cute pink bunny'. 'It reminds me that not everything is so serious,' she said. Alicia can play the guitar and piano. Her favourite colours are purple and blue.

★ Model **Jodie Kidd** was a showjumper as a child.

★ ★ ★ ★ THE A–Z OF CELEBRITY TRIVIA ★ ★ ★ ★

★ When she was younger, **Nicole Kidman** used to pray she would be turned into a witch. The reason? She fell in love with hit 60s US TV comedy *Bewitched*. Little did she know that one day she would land the lead role in the big-screen film of the same name. She is scared of butterflies. Her middle name? Mary. She also uses the name Miss Honey when booking into hotels.

★ Former MP and TV presenter **Robert Kilroy-Silk**'s father died in World War II. He has been quoted as saying, 'He died so that I could grow up in a free society, with the right to free speech to say what I like, when I like.' Kilroy bought Ozzy Osbourne's house in Buckinghamshire.

★ **Claire King**, star of *Bad Girls* and *Emmerdale*, changed her name to King in honour of her favourite musician, Elvis Presley.

★ Classical pianist and bikini-clad *I'm A Celebrity … Get Me Out of Here!* contestant **Myleene Klass** descends from six generations of classical musicians. Klass has been in love with astronomy for many years. She was one of the few people at the control centre of the touch-down of the UK Mars probe Beagle 2.

★ ★ ★ ★ THE A-Z OF CELEBRITY TRIVIA ★ ★ ★ ★

★ **Heidi Klum** is an avid painter and several of her works have appeared in US art magazines. The model is afraid of heights and has a fear of flying. When travelling, she carries her baby teeth in a pouch as good-luck charms. As part of German tradition, Heidi yodelled at her wedding to first husband Ric Pipino. Her legs are insured for $2 million.

★ British actress **Keira Knightley** was Queen Amidala's decoy in *Star Wars: Episode I*, although the film was promoted as if Natalie Portman played both roles. Among her talents are drawing, ballet and playing the flute and piano. Keira did her first nude scene at the age of sixteen in *The Hole*. She supports West Ham United FC. The *Atonement* and *Pirates of the Caribbean* star spent her first film pay packet on a doll's house. Keira's middle name is Christina.

★ Even though she appears in ads for Tommy Hilfiger's True Star fragrances, **Beyonce Knowles** is reportedly allergic to perfume. When performing at the 2004 Super Bowl, the diva had a few requests. Along with a VIP dressing room maintained at 78°F, the 22-year-old singer needed a 'private bathroom that's cleaned with disinfectant & anti-bacteria products before she arrives'. Foodwise, she wanted 'Juicy Baked Chicken: Legs, Wings & Breast only'. The poultry had to be seasoned

★ ★ ★ ★ THE A-Z OF CELEBRITY TRIVIA ★ ★ ★ ★

with 'fresh garlic, season salt, black pepper, and Cayenne pepper'. The pop princess spends £4,000 a week on a personal trainer to keep that stunning physique.

★ **John Krasinski**, who plays Jim Halpert in the American *Office*, can't stand Jell-O, but loves chocolate pudding.

★ Rocker **Lenny Kravitz** once kept a marijuana joint he'd shared with Mick Jagger for a year.

★ **Lisa Kudrow** has a degree in Sociobiology. She originally planned to be a doctor before going on to play Phoebe in *Friends*. Before landing the role, she had a part in *Frasier* but was sacked before filming commenced.

★ **Ashton Kutcher**, who is married to Demi Moore, has two webbed toes. The *What Happens in Vegas* actor helped pay his University of Iowa tuition fees by sweeping floors in a local General Mills plant. Ashton's older sister Tausha used to apply makeup on her sleeping brother when they were kids. When he fancies a drink, Ashton just loves homemade strawberry milkshakes with extra ice cream. He was turned down for the role of Batman in *Batman Begins* and the role of Superman in *Superman Returns*.

★ ★ ★ ★ THE A-Z OF CELEBRITY TRIVIA ★ ★ ★ ★

★ **Mark Lamarr**'s first record purchase was 'Jake the Peg' by Rolf Harris. The DJ and comedian is a member of the Boomtown Rats fanclub.

★ Model and photographer **Penny Lancaster**, the current Mrs Rod Stewart, wasn't always proud of her now famous figure. 'At school I towered over both boys and girls and was dreadfully skinny,' she recalled. 'I hated my 36-inch legs ... and would wear three pairs of thick tights to lend them bulk.' Little did she know that they would one day end up on the cover of one of Rod Stewart's albums.

★ *The Perfect Storm* actress **Diane Lane**'s mom, Colleen Farrington, was *Playboy*'s Miss October 1957 (the ex-playmate was also pregnant in one of her photo shoots).

★ For the 2007 Emmy Awards, *Heroes* star **Ali Larter** went without a hairstylist and displayed a self-done hairdo on the red carpet as part of Dove's Real Beauty campaign. The actress is frequently hounded by men about her infamous *Varsity Blues* whipped-cream bikini scene – Larter appeared in a saucy scene with cream covering her essential bits! Ali silences them by revealing that it was actually shaving cream: 'I really bursts their bubble ... [it] sounds so less appetising,' she says.

★ ★ ★ ★ THE A-Z OF CELEBRITY TRIVIA ★ ★ ★ ★

★ US singer **Avril Lavigne**'s middle name is Ramona. The pop princess learned how to use a Weedwacker at the age of 12 and once worked as a lawn landscaper. Most people don't know that she wrote the *Spongebob Squarepants* theme song. Her name means April the Vine when translated into French.

★ **Hugh Laurie** competed for Cambridge in the 1980 Oxford and Cambridge Boat Race. *House* star Hugh finished on the losing team.

★ *Alfie* star **Jude Law** bought two dogs, Porgy and Bess, which he gave as gifts to ex-girlfriend Sienna Miller. They were returned to him because she had no time to care for them. His parents run a fringe theatre company in France and his older sister Natasha is a highly regarded illustrator.

★ Celebrity chef **Nigella Lawson** comes from a high-profile family: former *Sunday Telegraph* editor Dominic Lawson is her brother and former Conservative Chancellor of the Exchequer Nigel Lawson, now Lord Lawson, is her father. She is also the sister-in-law of Lord Saatchi. Nigella failed her eleven plus exams because she refused to take the maths paper. She has her own kitchenware collection.

★ ★ ★ ★ THE A-Z OF CELEBRITY TRIVIA ★ ★ ★ ★

★ Millionaire actor **Matt LeBlanc** has not always been so solvent. At the time of his audition for *Friends* he was down to his last $50.

★ Duran Duran's **Simon Le Bon** often uses the name Shake Yabooty to check into hotels.

★ Rock band **Led Zeppelin** were once rumoured to have violated a groupie with a fish. The incident was mentioned in *Hammer of the Gods*, the sordid 1985 Led Zeppelin bio based on recollections of the band's then road manager Richard Cole.

★ Kung fu legend **Bruce Lee** was so fast that the film in his movies had to be slowed down to see his moves. He used to give Hollywood stars Steve McQueen, James Coburn and director Roman Polanski karate lessons.

★ **Christopher Lee** is an expert on JRR Tolkien and the only member of the cast of *Lord of the Rings* who had met Tolkien himself. Lee often visited the production department on the sets of the various *Lord of the Rings* movies to give advice and tips on the various attributes of the films.

★ Rocker **Tommy Lee** spent six months in jail for hitting Pamela Anderson, his then wife.

★ ★ ★ ★ THE A–Z OF CELEBRITY TRIVIA ★ ★ ★ ★

★ The late **Heath Ledger** and his sister Kate were given the names after the two characters in Emily Bronte's novel *Wuthering Heights*.

★ When **Vivien Leigh** was making the classic film *Gone with the Wind*, she complained that she did not like kissing Clark Gable because he had bad breath!

★ Beatle **John Lennon** was arrested with his wife Yoko Ono for marijuana possession. The charge nearly cost him the right to live in the US. Lennon was dyslexic. His favourite food was cornflakes. He shoplifted the harmonica he used on 'Love Me Do' in Holland.

★ US talk-show host **David Letterman** was, perhaps unsurprisingly, voted Class Smart Alec at school, Broad Ripple High.

★ English singer-songwriter and winner of the third series of *The X Factor* **Leona Lewis** wrote her first song at the age of 12. She planned to give music up altogether when she felt she wasn't getting anywhere, but her boyfriend persuaded her to audition for *The X Factor* and she won the competition, coming out with a £1 million recording contract. Lewis is vegetarian. She lives with her boyfriend Lou Al-Chamaa, an electrician. They met when she was ten years old.

★ ★ ★ ★ THE A–Z OF CELEBRITY TRIVIA ★ ★ ★ ★

★ **Shaznay Lewis** played football for Arsenal Ladies during her teenage years. All Saint Shaznay appeared in the 2002 film *Bend It Like Beckham* – she's the team captain and plays football in several scenes. She is a big fan of Missy Elliott.

★ US rapper **Lil' Kim** once spent £25,000 on clothes and Barbie dolls. The Queen of Bling's manicurist charges over £3,000 a day to wrap her nails in shredded $100 bills.

★ On her 26th birthday, *Lost* actress **Evangeline Lilly** brought a recycling bin to the show's set and begged the crew to start recycling as a birthday favour to her. When young, her fondness for climbing trees earned her the nickname of 'Monkey'.

★ *Match of the Day* presenter **Gary Lineker** was born on the 86th birthday of Winston Churchill, so was given Winston as his middle name.

★ *Charlie's Angels* and *Kill Bill* star **Lucy Liu** shares a birthday with Britney Spears. She is fluent in four languages and can play the accordion.

★ When auditioning for *The Sisterhood of the Travelling Pants*, **Blake Lively** walked into the room and simply

★ ★ ★ ★ **THE A-Z OF CELEBRITY TRIVIA** ★ ★ ★ ★

handed over her photo. The casting directors all thought she was joking at first, but, when she left the room without another word, they knew they'd found the Bridget they wanted.

★ Glamour model and *Celebrity Big Brother* contestant **Danielle Lloyd** is a former Miss England – she won in 2004. She was stripped of her title of Miss Great Britain 2006 after posing for nude pictures featured in *Playboy* magazine in December of that year. One of the judges on the panel for Miss Great Britain was footballer Teddy Sheringham, with whom she ended up having a relationship. When Danielle appeared on the BBC programme *Test the Nation*, she thought Winston Churchill was the first black president of the USA.

★ TV weathergirl **Sian Lloyd** appeared on the fourth series of the television show *The Apprentice* – recruited by a group of the young hopefuls not for anything weather-related, but to play a mother. Sian was as baffled by her selection as most of the viewers.

★ *Mean Girls* star **Lindsay Lohan** once rescued her youngest brother Dakota, whom she nicknames 'Codester', from drowning. She also collected Beanie Babies as a child and has almost every one.

★★★★ THE A-Z OF CELEBRITY TRIVIA ★★★★

★ *Desperate Housewives* star **Eva Longoria** learned to shoot at the age of five. She hunted deer, turkey, quail and wild pigs with her family at their Texas ranch. Eva's grandmother is disapproving of her *Desperate Housewives* sex scenes. She has yelled at her after watching her lusty rendezvous with the teenage gardener played by Jesse Metcalfe. Eva loves kickboxing, and has said she would like to go on a date with Brad Pitt. She was bullied when she was young for being ugly. Hard to believe, considering she is the only woman to have ever been number one on *Maxim's* 'Top 100 Hottest Female Stars' for two years running.

★ **Jennifer Lopez** is well known as a bit of a diva. When on tour, she requires a trailer at least 40 feet in length and everything in it must be white. This includes curtains, couches, candles, tablecloths, lilies and roses. Jennifer also likes a selection of current CDs and her three favourite scented candles from Diptyque – Tuberose, Figuier, and Heliotrope. Jennifer made demands for her trailer to be stocked with diet cream soda on the set of *Shall We Dance*. The fact that the drink is unavailable where the movie was being shot in Winnipeg, Canada, mattered little to the diva; supplies simply had to be flown in from Seattle in the USA. The star was spotted on the set eating

★ ★ ★ ★ THE A-Z OF CELEBRITY TRIVIA ★ ★ ★ ★

ice cream and strawberry muffins 'almost every day'. Super-market giant Tesco once christened a special curvaceous species of avocado 'J Lo'. Jenny from the Block was once turned down for a jeans advert due to the size of her bottom.

★ Former US porn star and now established actress **Traci Lords** appeared in *Penthouse* magazine when she was underage. She contributed to the Manic Street Preachers song 'Little Baby Nothing' in 1992.

★ Italian actress **Sophia Loren**'s first beauty contest prize included several rolls of wallpaper and a tablecloth with napkins. Sophia was initially considered for the role of Alexis in *Dynasty*, which Joan Collins eventually played. She has her own fragrance, Sophia.

★ Musician and actress **Courtney Love** was turned down for the parts of Marla Singer in *Fight Club*, Dorothy in *Jerry Maguire* and the lead role in *Moulin Rouge*.

★ **Jennifer Love Hewitt** sent Matt Damon an inflatable bed because she read he didn't feel like he has a bed of his own. She never heard back and now, he 'looks at me a little weird'.

★ ★ ★ ★ THE A-Z OF CELEBRITY TRIVIA ★ ★ ★ ★

★ It-girl **Daisy Lowe** discovered in 2004 that her father is Bush frontman and Gwen Stefani's beau Gavin Rossdale. She has been a model since the age of 15.

★ Former Powder singer and member of the Primrose Hill set **Pearl Lowe** has her own range of curtains, cushions and dresses. Her boyfriend is Supergrass drummer Danny Goffey and her daughter is London It-girl Daisy Lowe.

★ A childhood virus left actor **Rob Lowe** completely deaf in his right ear. 'No stereo for me,' he says. 'It's a mono world.'

★ **Andie MacDowell**, star of *Groundhog Day* and *Four Weddings and a Funeral*, worked at McDonalds and Pizza Hut in her youth.

★ **Shane MacGowan** was accepted into Westminster School, a posh English public school close to the Houses of Parliament. He was found in possession of drugs and was expelled in his second year. He went on to become the alcohol-fuelled frontman in The Pogues.

★ In 1979, **Shirley MacLaine** opted to use her time at the Oscar podium to cheer up her sibling, Warren

★ ★ ★ ★ THE A-Z OF CELEBRITY TRIVIA ★ ★ ★ ★

Beatty, who had lost out for *Heaven Can Wait*. 'I want to take this opportunity to say how proud I am of my little brother ... Just imagine what you could accomplish if you tried celibacy!' The cameras then panned to an embarrassed Beatty, who was sitting next to his equally awkward-looking date, Diane Keaton.

★ Australian supermodel **Elle Macpherson** was nicknamed Smelly Elly at school.

★ When **Richard Madeley**, of *Richard and Judy* fame, worked for Yorkshire Television he was nicknamed 'The Mannequin'. He once spent several minutes on air explaining about how he had been wrongly accused of shoplifting while interviewing Bill Clinton.

★ In 1989, **Madonna** signed an advertising deal with Pepsi. She debuted her new song 'Like a Prayer' in a Pepsi commercial and also made a separate music video for the song. The video was condemned by the Vatican and Pepsi dropped the commercial and allowed Madonna to keep her $5 million fee. These days, the singer likes to bang out a rendition of 'Truly Scrumptious' from *Chitty Chitty Bang Bang* to her children. Madonna is related to both Gwen Stefani and Celine Dion. Gwen's great-aunt's mother-in-law shares the same last name as Madonna Ciccone and is an

★ ★ ★ ★ THE A-Z OF CELEBRITY TRIVIA ★ ★ ★ ★

ancestor of Madonna's mother who was married to a distant relative of Celine's dad. When Madonna wed Guy Ritchie, the minister gave the couple a toilet roll each. When interviewed, Susan Brown said she gave the gift because 'the toilet rolls are long and strong, which is what I hope their marriage will be'. Madge used to work in the cloakroom of New York's Russian Tea Room restaurant, but she was fired for wearing fishnet stockings. The first time the singer appeared on David Letterman's show in the US she was bleeped for foul language a total of 12 times. She did better on her second appearance, being bleeped just the once.

★ *Kill Bill* actor **Michael Madsen** was considered for Woody Harrelson's role in *Natural Born Killers* and for the role of Marv in *Sin City*.

★ Spider-Man **Tobey Maguire** once fancied a career as a chef.

★ Controversial Mancunian stand-up comedian **Bernard Manning** did his National Service in the Military Police and one of his duties was guarding Albert Speer and Rudolf Hess in Spandau.

★ It is often said that Goth rocker **Marilyn Manson** played nerdy Paul Pfeiffer in late-80s sitcom *The*

Wonder Years, but he did not. Actor Josh Saviano played Kevin's best friend, and the ex-actor now works as a lawyer in New York. He was an only child.

★ Coldplay's **Chris Martin** says he is deeply influenced by the 'king of pop' Michael Jackson. Chris attributes his talent for falsetto singing to having observed the master. The singer is a vegetarian and has written songs for Jamelia.

★ Actor **Steve Martin** used to write songs for Sonny and Cher before he was famous.

★ Hollywood legend **Groucho Marx** didn't try bagels until he was 81.

★ Students' favourite **Rik Mayall** is left-handed.

★ *Wanted* star **James McAvoy** is a Glasgow Celtic FC supporter. Before he went into acting, he wanted to join the Navy, and before *that* he wanted to be a missionary. His dad is a builder and his mum is a nurse.

★ Before she went on to present *Big Brother*, **Davina McCall** was once a singing waitress in a Paris restaurant. She went to the same school as Kate Beckinsale and Nigella Lawson and in her late teens

★ ★ ★ ★ THE A-Z OF CELEBRITY TRIVIA ★ ★ ★ ★

she dated Eric Clapton, who was also a family friend. McCall appeared in the Kylie Minogue pop video for 'Word Is Out' and was the female voice dubber on one of the *Eurotrash* series in 1993. Davina is fluent in French and married to *Pet Rescue* presenter Matthew Robertson. Their three children were all born in the same month but in different years.

★ American actress and model – and lads' mag favourite – **Jenny McCarthy** has written a successful series of books on pregnancy and motherhood.

★ Beatles **Paul McCartney** and Ringo Starr are left-handed. In 1990, Paul spent nine days in the clink for possession of drugs in Japan. Paul wrote the Beatles song 'Martha my Dear' about his sheepdog.

★ In 1999, police responded to a noise complaint at 2.30am and found star of *How To Lose A Guy In Ten Days* **Matthew McConaughey** naked and playing the bongos.

★ Former *EastEnders* actress and singer **Martine McCutcheon** got her first role in an American advert – for the drink Kool-Aid – at the age of twelve. She was once in a girl band called Milan and also appeared in an Enya video in her youth.

★ ★ ★ ★ THE A-Z OF CELEBRITY TRIVIA ★ ★ ★ ★

★ Irish singer **Brian McFadden** worked as a security guard in McDonald's and as a bingo caller before finding fame with Westlife. He has five tattoos – on his back are two Chinese symbols saying 'love' and 'truth' sitting either side of a Peace sign, above which is the name 'Kerry', after his ex-wife Kerry Katona. Brian's fifth tat is on his inner left arm, and reads 'Sometimes life breaks in mysterious ways', a line from his song 'Sorry Love Daddy'. Brian was once awarded a gold card from Dublin kebab restaurant Abrakebabra for being their best customer.

★ Scottish actor **Ewan McGregor** has been teetotal since 2001, worrying that prior to this he was a borderline alcoholic. He has appeared nude in three different films and his older brother Colin is a pilot in the RAF.

★ **Coleen McLoughlin**, now Mrs Wayne Rooney, was born to Tony, a bricklayer who ran a boxing club, and Colette, a nursery nurse. At 16 Coleen revealed to her school yearbook that she planned on being 'famous and living a life of luxury' in ten years' time. Manchester United FC and England football star Wayne Rooney took the style icon to see *Austin Powers 2* on their first date. Wayne then proposed to McLoughlin on the forecourt of a BP garage in October 2003 when she

★ ★ ★ ★ THE A–Z OF CELEBRITY TRIVIA ★ ★ ★ ★

was 17, presenting her with a £46,500 diamond engagement ring. They now live in a £3.5 million mansion in Prestbury, Cheshire, complete with a cinema, gym and games room and American diner-themed kitchen. It also has seven plasma-screen TVs and a £30,000 state-of-the-art security system.

★ When on tour, **Meat Loaf**'s dressing room must contain a loaf of 100% multigrain bread (preferably Vogel's Flaxseed & Soy), two bags of potato chips, a package of low-fat chicken or turkey wieners, four Gala apples, four low-fat fresh-baked muffins, steamed broccoli and green beans, a sliced roast pork tenderloin, a sliced roast beef tenderloin and two baked potatoes. He doesn't require meatloaf.

★ **Leighton Meester**, who plays Blair Waldorf in *Gossip Girl*, is a published poet. Her surname is Dutch, and means 'Master' or 'Teacher'. *Gossip Girl* is filmed on the same stage at Silvercup Studios in New York that was occupied by *The Sopranos* for ten years.

★ *Have I Got News For You*'s **Paul Merton** is an only child.

★ Topless model **Melinda Messenger**'s career took off when she appeared in a double-glazing advertisement dressed only in lacy white knickers and a bra.

★ ★ ★ ★ THE A–Z OF CELEBRITY TRIVIA ★ ★ ★ ★

★ After a string of car accidents, singer **George Michael** employed a driver to ferry him around. His last performance with Wham! was on June 1986 at Wembley Stadium, and he is said to be worth around £70 million. Many years ago, he declined an invitation to play the character of a waiter in *Miami Vice*.

★ US actress and singer **Bette Midler** once worked as a pineapple chunker in a cannery in Hawaii.

★ Pop star and *Be Cool* actress **Christina Milian** once sold some of her possessions on eBay, with the proceeds to go to charity, and had to endure speculation that she was broke.

★ Model turned actress **Sienna Miller** is famous in America for upsetting the population of Pittsburgh by describing it as 'Shitsburgh' in an interview with *Rolling Stone* magazine. Sienna's birthday is one day before former partner Jude Law's. She was nicknamed 'Squit' – slang for unimportant person – at boarding school.

★ While attending Princeton, *Prison Break* star **Wentworth Miller** travelled the world performing with the school's acapella group, The Princeton Tigertones.

★ ★ ★ ★ THE A-Z OF CELEBRITY TRIVIA ★ ★ ★ ★

★ **Liza Minnelli** is the daughter of Judy Garland. Liza made her film debut at age 2½, in her mother's *In the Good Old Summertime*. At her wedding to fourth husband David Gest, best man duties were shared by Michael Jackson and brother Tito Jackson. The *Cabaret* star is the only Oscar winner with two Oscar-winning parents – her mum in 1939 and Dad Vincente Minnelli 1958.

★ *X Factor* judge **Dannii Minogue** performed on stage with her sister Kylie in 2006 for the first time in 19 years.

★ As of March 2008, **Kylie Minogue** had sold in excess of 60 million records. The word 'Kylie' is Aboriginal for boomerang. Kylie worked in a video shop before she was famous and, when the icon first appeared in *Neighbours*, her contract stated she was only to appear for a week.

★ While at convent school, **Dame Helen Mirren** set up a darts stall at a local fairground. The nuns from the convent got upset.

★ US hip-hop star **Missy Elliot** is a big fan of bio-degradable pants.

★ ★ ★ ★ THE A-Z OF CELEBRITY TRIVIA ★ ★ ★ ★

★ **Moby**'s real name is Richard Melville Hall. According to the musician, his middle name and the nickname 'Moby' were given to him by his parents because of his ancestral relationship *Moby Dick* author Herman Melville.

★ US actress **Marilyn Monroe**'s sexy wiggle wasn't only done for effect. She had bandy legs and weak ankles. She also used to bleach her pubic hair blonde. A longstanding rumour says that she had six toes on one foot. She was the first ever *Playboy* centrefold. The last line Marilyn ever spoke on film was 'How do you find your way back in the dark?' She said it to Clark Gable in *The Misfits*.

★ **Demi Moore** was born cross-eyed. US actress Moore, who has earned up to 20 million per movie, first found work as a bill collector. Demi and hubbie Ashton Kutcher once went to a Halloween party dressed as fellow stars (and couple at the time) Jennifer Lopez and Ben Affleck.

★ Diminutive actor and comedian **Dudley Moore** was born with a club foot.

★ Former Bond **Roger Moore** stipulates that he is provided with an unlimited amount of hand-rolled Cuban cigars in all of his film contracts.

★ ★ ★ ★ THE A–Z OF CELEBRITY TRIVIA ★ ★ ★ ★

★ *Britain's Got Talent* judge and former national newspaper editor **Piers Morgan** was named after racing driver Piers Courage. He first became editor of the *News of the World* at age 28.

★ Canadian singer–songwriter **Alanis Morissette** has a twin brother called Wade.

★ Lead singer of The Doors **Jim Morrison** was arrested for exposing himself on stage and using profanity. He was the first ever rock star to be arrested on stage. Mr Mojo Risin is an anagram of his name.

★ **Bob Mortimer**, comedian and one half of Vic and Bob, once had a trial for Middlesbrough FC.

★ Oscar-nominated British actress **Samantha Morton** left school at the age of thirteen.

★ Model **Kate Moss** has brown hair. She has been colouring her hair blonde since the beginning of her career. She is a vegan, and has confessed to drinking and smoking heavily at the age of 12.

★ Irish singer **Samantha Mumba** has a little dog called Foxy.

★ ★ ★ ★ THE A-Z OF CELEBRITY TRIVIA ★ ★ ★ ★

★ **Brittany Murphy** claims she started speaking at four-and-a-half months. She also says she was a very 'energetic child, really bubbly … extremely precocious'. The US actress was once the lead singer in a band called Blessed Soul. One of her first roles was in an advert for Skittles sweets.

★ Actor **Bill Murray** does not have an agent or a manager. He only considers offers for scripts and roles using a personal telephone number with a voice mailbox that he checks once in a while. In 1970 Bill dropped out of university after being arrested at Chicago's O'Hare Airport for trying to smuggle nearly 9 pounds of marijuana.

★ **Mike Myers**'s wedding ring is his late father's 1956 *Encyclopaedia Britannica* Salesman of the Year gift. The *Austin Powers* and *Shrek* star has two streets named after him in Toronto, Canada, and once starred in *The Littlest Hobo*. Mike is descended from William Wordsworth. He had bad acne as a teenager. Yeah Baby.

★ *Cold Feet* actor **James Nesbitt** originally planned to be a French teacher, and has said that his worst habit is thumb-sucking.

★ ★ ★ ★ THE A-Z OF CELEBRITY TRIVIA ★ ★ ★ ★

★ Acting legend and cooking-sauce king **Paul Newman** is colour blind. He was the oldest driver in the 1979 Le Mans 24-hour endurance race.

★ At age 37, **Jack Nicholson** discovered that the woman he'd always thought his sister was actually his mother. Jack was a bit of a bad boy at school – one year he was in detention every day! The Hollywood legend discovered the charms of beans on toast when serving it to his son and is now a self-confessed addict. He lost the role of Benjamin Braddock in *The Graduate* to Dustin Hoffman. He is an avid Los Angeles Lakers fan, and never misses a home game. Accordingly, producers on his films must work the shooting schedule around the Lakers' schedule. In 2007, Jack was voted the world's sexiest man over 50. He was 69.

★ US actor **Ed Norton**'s father invented the shopping mall.

★ Saucy comedian and chat-show host **Graham Norton** has appeared in *Brookside* as himself. The presenter used to perform stand-up comedy as Mother Teresa of Calcutta. His sister is actively involved in the Irish Green Party.

★ ★ ★ ★ THE A–Z OF CELEBRITY TRIVIA ★ ★ ★ ★

★ Singer **Sinead O'Connor**'s biggest hit 'Nothing Compares to You' was originally written by Prince.

★ Chat-show host **Paul O'Grady**, aka Lily Savage, used to be a social worker.

★ Cheeky television presenter **Dermot O'Leary** was once an altar boy.

★ Essex-boy-done-great **Jamie Oliver** once caught the eye of Tony Blair, who asked him to whip up an appropriately themed dinner for a meeting with the then PM's Italian counterpart. The result was such a success the Labour leader offered Jamie the job of 'food tsar' for Britain's hospitals, a role he declined. Both Nestle and Coca-Cola – who asked him to pose naked for an ad campaign – have also been rebuffed. Central to the ceremony at the chef's wedding to Jules was a performance by an Elvis impersonator who sang '*I Can't Help Falling In Love*'. The school-dinners campaigner is dyslexic and his parents own a pub called The Cricketers.

★ *T4* presenter **Miquita Oliver**'s mother is former Rip Rig & Panic singer Andrea Oliver. Miquita is friends with Lilly Allen and bites her (own!) nails.

★ ★ ★ ★ THE A-Z OF CELEBRITY TRIVIA ★ ★ ★ ★

★ Both **Olsen twins** had to wear fake teeth during the later years of *Full House* because their smiles began to look different. Ashley and Mary-Kate Olsen are not identical twins. Ashley is an inch shorter than Mary-Kate, and has a freckle above her lip. She is also right-handed, while Mary-Kate is a lefty. Ashley and Mary-Kate have a bi-monthly magazine called *Mary-Kate and Ashley Magazine*. The Olsen twins hate being referred to as the Olsen twins, as they feel it stops them being seen as individuals. They are billionaires.

★ **Jack Osbourne** has 'Mum' tattooed in a heart on his left shoulder as a thank you to Sharon, who helped him through his battle with drink and drugs. In Jack's autobiography, *21 Years Gone*, he speaks of being a child and watching his father Ozzy down pills. Trying to be just like his dad, Jack would buy Tic Tac mints and swallow them. Mum Sharon has banned him from going to South America because she fears he will be kidnapped by gangsters.

★ **Ozzy Osbourne** nearly murdered his wife Sharon in 1989, and was arrested for attempted murder, but charges were soon dropped. Ozzy and opera singer Sarah Brightman once shared the same vocal coach in London. He has a 12-metre water jet at his LA home to soak potential intruders, and has two smiley face

★ ★ ★ ★ THE A-Z OF CELEBRITY TRIVIA ★ ★ ★ ★

tattoos on his kneecaps. He talks to them when he's feeling lonely or sad.

★ **Sharon Osbourne** dropped out of school at age 15, saying that she was bored. When she was young she wanted to be a ballerina. Sharon was given a brand-new purple vacuum cleaner by Dyson to help clean up after her animals, after the television series *The Osbournes* aired. Not one to leave her domestic capabilities at that, she also used peanut oil – used to stop wooden countertops in her kitchen from drying out – to keep her hands soft.

★ *Lawrence of Arabia* made a star of **Peter O'Toole**, but only after Marlon Brando and Albert Finney turned the part down.

★ **P Diddy** has watched Al Pacino's *Scarface* film 63 times. He modelled in an advert at the age of two for Baskin-Robbins ice cream. The rapper has a personal barber who sketches out styles before even touching the hip-hop mogul's head.

★ While growing up, Canadian actress **Ellen Page** enjoyed playing with action figures and climbing trees. Page is prone to sleepwalking and hallucinating in her sleep. She named her dog Patti after Patti Smith.

★ ★ ★ ★ THE A-Z OF CELEBRITY TRIVIA ★ ★ ★ ★

★ EastEnder **Patsy Palmer** profited from Spice Girl Emma Bunton's failed audition for the part of Bianca Jackson in the soap.

★ US actress **Gwyneth Paltrow** was bullied at school because she was 'gawky'. Gwyneth used to spend Thanksgiving every year with Steven Spielberg and his wife before she was married. The star is not just an actress but something of a linguist too: she is fluent in Spanish, Italian and French. One of her children is called Apple. She lost out to Nicole Kidman for the role of Samantha in *Bewitched*.

★ **Hayden Panettiere**'s dogs are named Madison and Penny Lane. Hayden, who plays Claire in *Heroes*, has never been to acting school but she is an avid milk drinker.

★ *EastEnders* and *Strictly Come Dancing* star **Christopher Parker** was a stunt double in the film *Harry Potter and the Chamber of Secrets*.

★ *Sex and the City* star **Sarah Jessica Parker** grew up wearing 99-cent dresses and sharing clothes with her seven siblings. By the age of eight, Sarah, who had trained in singing and ballet, was already bringing home the pay cheques after making her TV debut in

★ ★ ★ ★ THE A-Z OF CELEBRITY TRIVIA ★ ★ ★ ★

The Little Match Girl. Sarah wore a Karl Lagerfeld-designed dress to the 2003 Emmy Awards that took 250 hours to make. Sarah once starred in a revival of *The Sound of Music* with four of her siblings. She had 15 outfit changes when she hosted the 2000 MTV Movie Awards, and was a UNICEF celebrity ambassador in Liberia.

★ Country-music icon **Dolly Parton** once entered a competition to impersonate herself. She lost. Dolly's breasts are insured for $600,000.

★ Opera legend **Pavarotti** used to demand that there be no noise backstage or distinct smells anywhere near him.

★ Lead singer of Wet Wet Wet **Marti Pellow** was born in a public toilet.

★ In 1987, actor **Sean Penn** spent a month in jail for hitting a man who had kissed Madonna, who he was married to at the time.

★ **Matthew Perry** is missing part of his middle finger on his right hand due to a door-shutting accident. The *Friends* star was ranked number 2 at tennis in Ottawa at the age of 13.

★ ★ ★ ★ THE A–Z OF CELEBRITY TRIVIA ★ ★ ★ ★

★ *Goodfellas* star **Joe Pesci** was once lead vocalist for Joey Dee and The Starliters.

★ Catwoman **Michelle Pfeiffer** once worked as a supermarket assistant. At school, she was bullied because of her big lips. Michelle was Oscar-nominated for her role in *The Fabulous Baker Boys*, but only after Madonna and Debra Winger turned the part down.

★ 'Royal Rebel' **Zara Phillips** has a pierced tongue.

★ **Nick Pickard**, who plays Tony Hutchinson in *Hollyoaks*, is currently the longest-serving cast member and starred in the very first episode in 1995. He made an appearance in the Steven Spielberg film *Empire Of The Sun*.

★ Every time US pop star **Pink** releases a new album, she takes a bottle of champagne to New York's Virgin Megastore to buy the first copy. Virgin's alcohol-in-store policy was unavailable at the time of going to press. She has won two Grammy Awards. Pink proposed to her motocross racer Carey Hart by holding up a sign at one of his races that read 'Will you marry me?' She is a strict vegetarian who once protested against the use of real fur in the bearskins of the Queen's guard's caps.

★ ★ ★ ★ THE A-Z OF CELEBRITY TRIVIA ★ ★ ★ ★

★ *Dr Who* actress **Billie Piper** started dance classes at the age of five and just two years later was filming soft-drink commercials for American TV. She even appeared as an extra alongside Madonna in *Evita*. Her big break came as she entered her teens, when she was picked to star in a TV commercial for the pop bible *Smash Hits*. All she had to do was run up to the camera, blow a pink bubblegum bubble and shout 'Pop!' At just 15, Billie became the youngest female to top the charts in almost 40 years with her number-one hit 'Because We Want To'. On meeting her, DJ Chris Evans fell in love and bought Billie a Ferrari – even though she had yet to pass her driving test – which he filled with long-stemmed roses. He told his listeners that he had met the girl he was going to marry. Even though they are divorced, they remain great friends. Billie has two tattoos: a star shape on her right wrist and 'Mr Fox' on her left. Her husband Lawrence Fox has a 'Mrs Fox' tattoo.

★ **Brad Pitt** belonged to the Key Club and the Forensics Club in high school, and before he became an actor he supported himself as a chauffeur, a furniture mover and a costumed chicken mascot for a restaurant, El Pollo Loco. Brad had acne as a teenager, and the scars have been removed by dermabrasion. He is banned from entering China because of his role in *Seven Years in*

★ ★ ★ ★ THE A-Z OF CELEBRITY TRIVIA ★ ★ ★ ★

Tibet. Brad came top of a survey asking which celebrity women considered to be the most well endowed, conducted by American condom makers Trojan.

★ *Grey's Anatomy* star **Ellen Pompeo** wanted to be an archaeologist when she was young. She earns around $200,000 per episode of the hit drama series. She was introduced to her husband, Chris Ivery, at a Whole Foods Market store in Los Angeles.

★ Former Tory MP **Michael Portillo** featured in a Ribena advert as a child.

★ *Star Wars* actress **Natalie Portman** has been a vegetarian since childhood.

★ King of rock'n'roll **Elvis Presley**'s middle name is Aron, in honour of his twin brother Garon, who died at birth. Elvis failed his music class at school and never once played an encore. His favourite food was fried peanut butter and banana sandwiches; he weighed 230 pounds and had ten different drugs in his body at the time of his death. His hip-wiggling started out as a stage fright. He was so nervous that his legs would shake.

★ American actress **Priscilla Presley** became a mother again after becoming a grandmother.

★ ★ ★ ★ THE A-Z OF CELEBRITY TRIVIA ★ ★ ★ ★

★ In 2005, doctors told purple-loving pop star **Prince** that he would need a hip replacement from his years of dancing. The diminutive star claims to have made something in the region of 50 music videos for songs that have never been released. He was at various times during the 1990s known as O(+> and The Artist before settling his dispute with his record company in 2000 and going back to plain old Prince. In 2007, he played 21 dates in London alone.

★ **Prince Charles** gave recovering alcoholic Ozzy Osbourne a bottle of whisky after his quad-bike crash. The prince used the chat-up line 'I like to give myself heirs' when he was at Cambridge University, and he was named 'Hooligan of the Year' by the RSPCA for hunting wild boar abroad.

★ **Princess Diana** was the first royal bride not to have the word 'obey' in her wedding vows. She was also a keen tap dancer.

★ Hollywood star **Freddie Prince Jr**, Sarah Michelle Gellar's beau, plucks his eyebrows to avoid comparisons with Bert from *Sesame Street*. He likes martial arts and tap dancing.

★ ★ ★ ★ THE A-Z OF CELEBRITY TRIVIA ★ ★ ★ ★

★ *Harry Potter* actor **Daniel Radcliffe** doesn't read any articles about himself or his movies. He doesn't like cockroaches either, and it is rumoured that he can rotate his arm 360 degrees. He is a big fan of wrestling and The Rock is his favourite wrestler.

★ Cricketer and former *Strictly Come Dancing* winner **Mark Ramprakash** supports Arsenal and his favourite television programme is *CSI Las Vegas*.

★ **Gordon Ramsay** was awarded the 2007 Chef of the Year award at the *GQ* Men of the Year Awards. The celebrity chef and restaurateur runs the London marathon every year. The foul-mouthed chef was once a professional footballer with Glasgow Rangers FC.

★ Sugababe **Heidi Range** was a member of the original Atomic Kitten line-up.

★ Actor and director **Robert Redford** was the first choice to star in *The Graduate*, but Dustin Hoffman made his name in the role when Redford turned it down.

★ The late **Christopher Reeve** wasn't the first choice to play Superman. Paul Newman, Robert Redford and Steve McQueen all turned down the role before him.

★ ★ ★ ★ THE A-Z OF CELEBRITY TRIVIA ★ ★ ★ ★

★ *Matrix* star **Keanu Reeves**'s first name is Hawaiian for 'cool breeze over the mountains'. He once managed a pasta shop in Toronto. Throughout the 1990s, Keanu was the subject of a false rumour that he had married American executive David Geffen. Keanu's father has done time in prison for cocaine possession.

★ He used to be a pig farmer, then he became a famous comedian. The name? **Vic Reeves**.

★ *American Pie* star **Tara Reid** likes to check into hotels with the name Strawberry Shortcake. She attended high school in New Jersey with *American Idol* contestant Constantine Maroulis. Tara was the first person ever to appear on multiple covers of *Maxim* magazine. She is a fashion consultant to her brother Patrick's clothes store and she has a dog named Tequila.

★ Rapper **Busta Rhymes** insists that there is no pork or beef anywhere near his dressing room; but he does like a 24-piece bucket of KFC.

★ US actress **Christina Ricci** has admitted that she loves gambling. Her father is a lawyer, though previously he worked as a psychiatrist specialising in shrieking therapy. Christina has never had formal acting training. She was turned down for two roles opposite Leonardo

★ ★ ★ ★ THE A-Z OF CELEBRITY TRIVIA ★ ★ ★ ★

DiCaprio including Juliet in *Romeo and Juliet*, and Rose in *Titanic*.

★ Veteran singer **Sir Cliff Richard** owns a vineyard. Adega do Canto is the winery that produces Sir Cliff's wine, Vida Nova.

★ Bond girl and reality-TV star **Denise Richards** craved French toast and grapefruit during her first pregnancy and rubbed coconut butter cream on her belly to avoid stretch marks. As a child, she was nicknamed 'fish lips' due to her pout.

★ Rolling Stone **Keith Richards**'s third finger of his left hand is insured for a whopping £1 million.

★ **Nicole Richie** gave her *Simple Life* co-star Paris Hilton a rat called Tori Spelling for Christmas one year.

★ **Shane Richie** says his worst job was cleaning up after donkeys when he was 17 and running donkey derbys. Actor and comedian Shane used to use the stage name Shane Skywalker. He changed his name to Ritchie following advice from fellow performer Lenny Henry.

★ Director **Guy Ritchie** once kicked a fan who was lurking around his house, and received a police caution

★ ★ ★ ★ **THE A-Z OF CELEBRITY TRIVIA** ★ ★ ★ ★

for his trouble. At the last of the ten schools he attended, the director was expelled for allegedly dabbling in drugs and – probably as a result of not being diagnosed as dyslexic until later – completed his formal education with little more than a GCSE in film studies.

★ Pretty Woman **Julia Roberts** had her own scent created, at a cost of £4,000/litre, for the Oscars one year. The Hollywood beauty's middle name is Fiona. Her left eye tears up when she gets nervous. Presumably she doesn't get nervous when her bank manager calls, as she is the highest-paid actress in film history.

★ Girls Aloud star **Nicola Roberts** was the second member of the band to be selected on *Popstars: The Rivals*. She was originally eliminated before the final stage, but, after another contestant pulled out of the show, because of the contract on offer, she was brought back into the final ten. Her nickname is Cola and she has co-written two Girls Aloud tracks. Nicola is the youngest member of the group and she is the creator of make-up range Dainty Doll.

★ *The Weakest Link* host and millionaire **Anne Robinson**'s maths teacher told her she 'would never make anything of herself'.

★ ★ ★ ★ THE A-Z OF CELEBRITY TRIVIA ★ ★ ★ ★

★ Hollywood legends **Ginger Rogers** and Rita Hayworth were cousins.

★ Brazilian footballer **Ronaldinho** once smashed a window at a 12th-century cathedral after fluffing an overhead kick when filming an advert.

★ Footballer **Cristiano Ronaldo**'s name was inspired by his father's favourite actor Ronald Reagan.

★ Hip producer **Mark Ronson** got his first instrument – a drum kit – at the age of five. He was the DJ at the wedding of Tom Cruise and Katie Holmes.

★ Footballer **Wayne Rooney**'s favourite film is *Grease*, and his favourite TV series is *Only Fools and Horses*. He loves reading *Harry Potter*.

★ **Axl Rose**, lead singer of Guns n' Roses, had his own dressing room whenever the band went on tour in the 80s and 90s, and he was very specific about what should be contained in it. Firstly, there was water and honey, then a rib-eye steak dinner; a large pepperoni pizza; a deli tray with a heavy emphasis on lean roast beef, ham and turkey; and a bottle of Dom Perignon.

★ ★ ★ ★ THE A–Z OF CELEBRITY TRIVIA ★ ★ ★ ★

★ TV presenter **Gaby Roslin** is wheat intolerant. She gave it up and it helped to cure her insomnia.

★ **Jonathan Ross** has appeared in television commercials for Rice Krispies, Pizza Hut and Harp Lager. Presenter Jonathan married his wife Jane Goldman in Las Vegas.

★ *Reservoir Dogs'* Mr Orange **Tim Roth** has pierced nipples.

★ **JK Rowling**'s *Harry Potter* books have been translated into 42 languages, and have sold more than 325 million copies worldwide, and the success of the franchise has made its creator thus far the only billionaire author in existence. The bestselling author-to-be wrote her first story, *Rabbit*, when she was just five years old. Rowling has no middle name. The 'K' was suggested by her literary agent, who thought it would be best if the author was known by initials rather than her real name Kathleen. The reason? He was worried that boys would not read a book written by a woman, but didn't think J Rowling was enough.

★ Actress **Keri Russell**'s nickname is Care Bear.

★ ★ ★ ★ THE A-Z OF CELEBRITY TRIVIA ★ ★ ★ ★

★ US actor **Kurt Russell**, long-time partner of Goldie Hawn, quit acting in 1971 to try to pursue a career in minor-league baseball.

★ *When Harry Met Sally* star **Meg Ryan**'s real name is Margaret Hyra. She worked as a journalist before becoming famous.

★ Quirky US actress **Winona Ryder**'s real name is Winona Horowitz. Winona is really a blonde.

★ Comic actor **Adam Sandler** has two dogs. Their names are Matzoball and Meatball. Adam's nickname is Sandman.

★ Former *T4* presenter **June Sarpong** has written for the *Guardian* newspaper, interviewed then Prime Minister Tony Blair and been awarded an MBE during her career.

★ The absolutely fabulous **Jennifer Saunders** attended the Central School of Speech and Drama in London. She and Dawn French declined an OBE in 2001. She and Dawn also shared a flat at the start of their careers in comedy.

★ Veteran DJ and marathon runner **Jimmy Saville** was a coalminer before he was famous.

★ ★ ★ ★ THE A-Z OF CELEBRITY TRIVIA ★ ★ ★ ★

★ Nice work if you can get it: supermodel **Claudia Schiffer** pocketed £200,000 for a one-minute appearance alongside Hugh Grant in *Love Actually*.

★ Formula One Champion **Michael Schumacher** was so overwhelmed at the birth of his first child, daughter Gina Marie, he thought he would faint.

★ *The Darjeeling Limited* star **Jason Schwartzman** was a member of the band Phantom Planet, who later provided the theme song for television series *The O.C.*

★ **Arnold Schwarzenegger** paid $772,500 for President John F Kennedy's golf clubs at an auction in 1996, four years after he bought the first civilian Hummer vehicle. Part of Arnie's fee for appearing in *Terminator 2* was a Gulf Stream GIII jet aircraft. In his first screen role, the Italian TV film *Hercules in New York*, he was credited as Arnold Strong.

★ **David Schwimmer** went to Beverly Hills High School, the school that was the inspiration for TV series *Beverly Hills 90210*. His *Friends* character Ross had a monkey but it was fired for puking worms during filming.

★ ★ ★ ★ THE A–Z OF CELEBRITY TRIVIA ★ ★ ★ ★

★ Action-movie veteran **Steven Seagal** is, in fact, the real deal. He's a seventh degree Black Belt in Akido.

★ American comedian **Jerry Seinfeld** was once paid £315,000 for a 15-minute gig in Las Vegas. That's £21,000 a minute.

★ Pop star **Shaggy** was once a US Marine and served in the first Gulf War.

★ The late **Tupac Shakur**'s shaven hairstyle was less a style statement than a force of nature. He was suffering from premature baldness.

★ *Platoon* and *Wall Street* star **Charlie Sheen** married Donna Peel in 1995. They had only known each other six weeks.

★ US actress **Brooke Shields** can trace her lineage back to Henry IV of France and Lucrezia Borgia. Costumers on the set of *The Blue Lagoon* glued Brooke's long-haired wig to her breasts so that they wouldn't show during her topless scenes. At 15, Brooke became the youngest person ever to host *The Muppet Show*, playing Alice in the Muppets' take on *Alice in Wonderland*.

★ ★ ★ ★ THE A–Z OF CELEBRITY TRIVIA ★ ★ ★ ★

★ An anagram of US actress **Alicia Silverstone** is 'Evil Lass In Erotica'. Far from evil, the Hollywood star is a vegan. She was voted the world's sexiest female vegetarian celebrity by PETA (People for the Ethical Treatment of Animals). She is fluent in French and her parents are English. The first advertisement she ever appeared in was for Domino's Pizza.

★ Pop group **Simply Red** are so named because they support Manchester United FC.

★ Singer and actress **Ashlee Simpson** owns a dog named Blondie. The lovely Ashlee was offered $4 million to pose for *Playboy* magazine but turned the offer down. Her song 'Catch Me When I Fall' was written about her bad experience on *Saturday Night Live*.

★ **Jessica Simpson**'s father is a former Baptist minister. He once credited his daughter's breasts with forging her sex-symbol status. 'You can't cover those suckers up!' he said. At age 12, the singer and actress auditioned for *The Mickey Mouse Club* and got to the finals. At the age of 14, she released a self-titled gospel album. When she was 16, the pop star tried to adopt a Mexican baby found in a dumpster. While running with a gun during the filming of *Major Movie Star*, Jessica tripped and

★ ★ ★ ★ THE A-Z OF CELEBRITY TRIVIA ★ ★ ★ ★

broke her nose. Simpson once donated a Chrysler van to an orphanage in Nuevo Laredo.

★ Controversial US football player and actor **OJ Simpson** was considered to play the role of the Terminator in the blockbuster movie, but producers rejected him as they thought he would not be taken seriously.

★ Comedian and well-known football fan **Frank Skinner** was expelled from school over a money-making school-meal scam. He was born Chris Collins, and pinched his stage name from a bloke at his local domino club. Frank is teetotal and only learned to swim as an adult.

★ There were 5000 hopefuls for the job of hostess on *Wheel of Fortune*, but **Carol Smillie** came out on top.

★ Model **Anna Nicole Smith** used to demand Godiva chocolates at every *Guess* shoot in the early 90s. When asked to name an aphrodisiac, she once replied 'Anna Nicole Smith.' The busty blonde married billionaire Howard J Marshall when she was 26 and he was 89. She was the tallest, heaviest and possessor of the biggest measurements of any of the *Playboy* 'Playmates of the Year'.

★ ★ ★ ★ THE A-Z OF CELEBRITY TRIVIA ★ ★ ★ ★

★ *GM:TV* newsreader **Penny Smith** once had a fan-run website called 'Penny from Heaven'. She is a big fan of folk-singer John Martyn.

★ Hollywood favourite **Will Smith** is one of many Hollywood parents to buy Posh Tots' mini mansions, castles and chalets for his children to play in. Prices start at £29,375 for the little homes. Will's first ever day of acting was the first episode of *The Fresh Prince of Bel Air*. Will loves to play chess. He speaks fluent Spanish and was nicknamed 'Prince' because he is able to charm his way out of anything.

★ Rap star **Snoop Dogg** was the first recording artist ever to enter the US charts at number one with a debut record – 1993's *Doggystyle*. He has been denied entry to both the UK and Australia in the past and he is a big fan of the band *Metallica*.

★ Newsreader **Jon Snow** was booted out of Liverpool University for organising an anti-apartheid demonstration.

★ **Kevin Spacey** was a stand-up comedian before he became an actor. *American Beauty* star Kevin burned his sister's tree house down when they were children. Later, his parents decided to send him to military school.

★ ★ ★ ★ THE A-Z OF CELEBRITY TRIVIA ★ ★ ★ ★

★ **The Spice Girls** were originally called Touch. As the Spice Girls, they sold over 50 million records worldwide with only three albums. Their aliases Scary, Baby, Ginger, Posh and Sporty were given by *Top of the Pops* Magazine. 'Wannabe' was shot in St Pancras Chambers, London. Tickets for The Return of the Spice Girls London concert sold out in 38 seconds and the band mantra – Girl Power – has even made the *Oxford English Dictionary*.

★ At school, **Steven Spielberg** was nicknamed 'the retard', and once lost a race to a boy in the class who was actually mentally retarded. The first episode of *Columbo* was directed by Steven.

★ Singer **Dusty Springfield** once won damages over a television sketch portraying her as a drunk. She sued over a scene in which impressionist Bobby Davro lurched on stage wearing a blonde wig and pretended to fall down.

★ The first song **Bruce Springsteen** was able to strum on his guitar was 'It's All Over Now', by the Rolling Stones. The rocker's voice is insured for $6 million.

★ *Rocky* star **Sylvester Stallone** worked as a lion-cage sweeper in Central Park Zoo, New York, when he was

★ ★ ★ ★ **THE A-Z OF CELEBRITY TRIVIA** ★ ★ ★ ★

a struggling actor. His mother Jackie claims her dogs predicted George Bush's victory in the US election. At school, Sylvester was voted 'Most Likely to End Up in an Electric Chair' by his classmates.

★ Madcap comedian and impressionist **Freddie Starr** used so much Valium to cope with his stage fright that he became addicted to the stuff.

★ **Ringo Starr** can't swim and received more fan mail than any other Beatle. Ringo is Japanese for apple sauce, and the star appeared in a Japanese advert for that very product in 1996.

★ **Gwen Stefani** admits that she's had only two boyfriends in her life: No Doubt band mate Tony Kanal and husband Gavin Rossdale. Gwen arrived an hour late to her wedding. She loves Sushi. She is a distant cousin of Madonna, and she is a Catholic.

★ Former S Club 7 singer **Rachel Stevens** has a pierced navel.

★ Hollywood legend **James Stewart** had it written into each of his film contracts that he was able to choose the hats he wore on screen.

★ ★ ★ ★ THE A-Z OF CELEBRITY TRIVIA ★ ★ ★ ★

★ **Rod Stewart** was a gravedigger before he became a famous rock star. Rod's voice is insured for $6 million. The veteran rocker is football mad. He had an apprenticeship with Brentford FC before he was famous and he has a full-size football pitch on the grounds of his home in the UK.

★ Frat Pack funnyman **Ben Stiller** holds the Razzie Awards – the anti-Oscars, celebrating the worst of Hollywood for the year – record for most nominations in one year. In 2004, he was nominated for Worst Actor in five of the six films in which he appeared: *Along Came Polly*, *Starsky & Hutch*, *Anchorman: The Legend of Ron Burgundy*, *Dodgeball: A True Underdog Story* and *Envy*. His sixth film, which didn't make the cut, was *Meet the Fockers*. His favourite actress of all time is Diane Keaton. Ben and wife Christine Taylor have both made guest appearances in sitcom *Friends*. Not in the same episode though, and he received no awards, Razzie-style or otherwise, for his performance.

★ **Sting** is film star Leonardo DiCaprio's next-door neighbour. Sting's real name is Gordon Sumner, and the name Sting came about because of a yellow and black shirt he used to wear – people thought he looked like a bee!

★ ★ ★ ★ THE A–Z OF CELEBRITY TRIVIA ★ ★ ★ ★

★ Clever clogs **Sharon Stone** is a member of MENSA and has an IQ of 150. She was Miss Crawford County in 1976.

★ *The Devil Wears Prada* star **Meryl Streep** lost the lead role in *Evita* to Madonna.

★ Diva **Barbra Streisand** had a black microphone spray-painted white on the *Oprah Winfrey Show* so that it matched her off-white outfit. Streisand has made more gold and platinum albums than any other solo female artist, and she once performed dressed as a chocolate chip cookie.

★ Saucy nightclub owner **Peter Stringfellow** was found guilty of selling stolen goods when he was twenty, and spent a few days in prison for his offence. These days he's known either as Britain's best-loved playboy or just simply as 'Mr Notorious'.

★ English entrepreneur, businessman and star of *The Apprentice* **Sir Alan Sugar** comes from the East End of London and is the youngest son of Nathan Sugar, a tailor. Ask him to be fair and you're likely to receive the following reply: 'Fair? The only fair you're gonna get is your bloody train fare!' and 'Tell me, why shouldn't I fire you?'

★ ★ ★ ★ THE A-Z OF CELEBRITY TRIVIA ★ ★ ★ ★

★ Hollywood bad boy and star of *24* **Kiefer Sutherland** has six tattoos, including his family's Scottish crest on his back. Kiefer can play both the violin and the guitar. He began learning to play the violin aged five and the guitar aged 12.

★ When she was a child, *Million Dollar Baby* star **Hilary Swank** lived with her mum in a car. She enjoys knitting in her free time.

★ Dirty Dancer **Patrick Swayze**'s first crush was on original Charlie's Angel Jaclyn Smith. His mother gave her dance classes. During his school years Patrick's hobbies included classical ballet and ice skating, but Patrick was bullied over the ballet dancing. He took the lead role of Prince Charming in *Disney on Ice*. He has been voted the 'Sexiest Man Alive' in *People* magazine and he breeds Arabian horses.

★ *Kill Bill* director **Quentin Tarantino** had the bar from the set of the House of Blue Leaves in the film installed in his own home.

★ DJ and TV presenter **Chris Tarrant** is an only child.

★ British screen legend **Elizabeth Taylor**'s husband, Eddie Fisher, was paid $1,500 a day to make sure that she

★ ★ ★ ★ THE A-Z OF CELEBRITY TRIVIA ★ ★ ★ ★

arrived on time while making the film *Cleopatra*. Years later, a gown she wore in 1969 would reach £98,000 at auction. Elizabeth has graced the cover of *Life* magazine more than any other person, and was a competitor of Joan Collins for the role of Alexis in *Dynasty*.

★ US child actress **Shirley Temple** always had exactly 56 curls in her hair. She had made her first million by the age of ten.

★ TV presenter and radio DJ **Jamie Theakston** was once the goalkeeper in a celebrity charity football match where English celebrities were up against ex-footballers. Jamie tried to save a penalty from Argentinean Diego Maradona but failed to do so.

★ Struggling actress **Charlize Theron** landed her first agent in a bank. He signed her after witnessing her throwing a fit at a bank teller who refused to cash her cheque. Her surname is pronounced in Afrikaans as 'Teronn', although she prefers the pronunciation 'Thrown'. Charlize, whose first language is Afrikaans, lost her South African accent by watching hours of TV and singing along with American songs on the radio.

★ TV chef **Antony Worrall Thompson** swam the English Channel when he was 16.

★ ★ ★ ★ THE A-Z OF CELEBRITY TRIVIA ★ ★ ★ ★

★ US film star and former beau of Angelina Jolie **Billy Bob Thornton** once spent 18 months working in a Los Angeles pizza parlour. He made it to assistant manager. He has a phobia of clowns.

★ TV presenter **Kate Thornton** was the youngest ever editor of *Smash Hits* magazine at the age of 21.

★ *Kill Bill* star **Uma Thurman**'s middle name is Karuna. Her father was the first Westerner to be ordained a Tibetan Buddhist monk. Her parents named her Uma after a Hindu goddess. Her chow chow dog is called Muffy.

★ Former 'N Sync singer **Justin Timberlake** sold out his 2003 Christmas show in Ireland in 40 seconds flat. His celebrity friends include Will.i.am from Black Eyed Peas, uber-producer Timbaland and Coldplay frontman Chris Martin. Justin's big break was on *The Mickey Mouse Club*. At age 10, he won 1991 pre-teen Mr America pageant. The following year, he became the first male winner of America's Universal Charm pageant. The pop star helped revive the fortunes of fast-food giant McDonalds when his 'I'm Lovin' It' song was used in television adverts. It is thought that he was paid $6 million for the campaign.

★ ★ ★ ★ THE A–Z OF CELEBRITY TRIVIA ★ ★ ★ ★

★ It-girl **Tara Palmer Tomkinson** is a concert pianist who has played to audiences at the Royal Albert Hall. Her father was an Olympic skier. Tara worked in banking when she left school.

★ *Royle Family* actor **Ricky Tomlinson** spent two years in jail for his role in the 1972 builders' strike. He was in solitary confinement for most of his sentence.

★ **John Travolta** is not the man walking down the street at the start of *Saturday Night Fever*. The legs belong to his stand-in, Jeff Zinn. John was cast in *Pulp Fiction* only because Michael Madsen, who had a major role in Tarantino's previous film *Reservoir Dogs*, turned it down. Travolta is famous for turning down two plum roles – in *An Officer and a Gentleman* and *American Gigolo* – which Richard Gere took. John became a member of the mile-high club with wife Kelly Preston while on a flight back to America from their wedding in France.

★ Fashion advisers **Trinny and Susannah** have consulted around 5,000 women on their outfits. They met at Viscount Linley's dinner party and initially disliked each other.

★ Former cricketer **Phil Tufnell** gave up his career in the sport to appear on *I'm a Celebrity … Get Me Out of Here!*

★★★★ THE A–Z OF CELEBRITY TRIVIA ★★★★

★ **Jethro Tull** was an English horticulturist. It is also the name of a band, not a solo artist; the singer was Ian Anderson.

★ Soap star **Lacey Turner** first auditioned for the part of Demi on *EastEnders* before being chosen for the part of Stacey Slater. She loves garage and R'n'B and is fan of Dizzee Rascal.

★ Annie Mae Bullock might not be a household name, but that's only because she changed it to **Tina Turner**. Tina's legs are insured for $3.2 million.

★ Canadian songstress **Shania Twain** began her career as a secretary.

★ Actress **Liv Tyler** is dyslexic and owns a dog called Neal. She is also a vegetarian. Liv was named after Liv Ullmann, a Norwegian actress and muse to Ingmar Bergman.

★ **U2**'s sound system on tour weighs 30 tonnes.

★ **Keith Urban**, country singer and husband of Nicole Kidman, does not know how to read music. He loves sushi and sang backing vocals on the INXS song 'Shining Star'.

★ ★ ★ ★ THE A-Z OF CELEBRITY TRIVIA ★ ★ ★ ★

★ **Usher** holds the *Star Search* record for the longest note by a child: 12.1 seconds.

★ Former *Neighbours* star and pop singer **Holly Valance**'s real surname is Vuckadinovic. Holly is related to the late Benny Hill. Her grandfather was Benny's cousin.

★ Hollywood actor **Jean-Claude Van Damme** – aka The Muscles from Brussels – wasn't just an onscreen tough guy: he competed in full-contact karate tournaments during the 1980s and only ever lost one bout. When Jean-Claude started acting, controversy dogged his claims to being a karate champion as no footage of his fights could be found. The explanation was rather straightforward: Van Damme competed under his real name, Jean-Claude Van Varenberg.

★ Rock band **Van Halen** gained notoriety for their demand that, at every gig, their dressing room was to contain a large bowl of M&M's, but with all the brown ones removed. This was seen as a reflection of their egos, but the idea was actually dreamed up by tour promoters as an easy way of checking if the concert venues had read the contract properly. If there were no brown M&M's, the band could be sure that the organisers were actually paying attention to their detailed technical and safety specifications.

★ ★ ★ ★ THE A-Z OF CELEBRITY TRIVIA ★ ★ ★ ★

★ TV presenter **Denise Van Outen** made a royal blunder when she stole an ashtray and a tissue-box holder from Buckingham Palace. She got caught, and handed the goods back to the Queen with a sincere apology. Denise was once a model for a knitting publication when she was only seven. As a student, she appeared in the chorus of *Les Misérables* with fellow Sylvia Young student Melanie Blatt, of All Saints.

★ Radio and television presenter **Johnny Vaughan** was born at the precise moment that England scored the winning goal in the 1966 World Cup Final. Johnny's pet bulldog, Harvey, once crashed his £60,000 sports car when he jumped across the seat and knocked the gear stick into 'drive'. In 1988, Johnny was arrested for trying to sell £15,000 of cocaine to undercover policemen. He was found guilty of being 'concerned with the supply' of cocaine and sentenced to four years in prison. He served two of them. Johnny met his wife Antonia Davies in a video store when he was 19. He owns several cars including a Maserati 3200 GT.

★ Larger-than-life comedian **Johnny Vegas** was once a Butlins Redcoat. He studied art and ceramic design at university, and at one point wanted to be a potter. He gave up when he received a third-class degree. Possibly hurt by *OK!* and *Hello!* magazines' lack of interest, the

★ ★ ★ ★ THE A-Z OF CELEBRITY TRIVIA ★ ★ ★ ★

comedian sold his wedding photographs to *Viz* magazine for one pound.

★ **Carol Vorderman**'s school report noted that she had 'a masterly hold over maths which could prove profitable later on'. Carol's mum saw an advert for a mathematician on *Countdown* and applied for the job for her.

★ Actor **Christopher Walken** manages to insert a little dance number into nearly all of his roles, no matter how small.

★ *Little Britain* star **David Walliams** met comedy partner Matt Lucas in 1990 at the National Youth Theatre. They were grouped together because they were both so good at impressions.

★ *Private Practice* star **Kate Walsh** is naturally blonde, but she normally dyes her hair red for her acting roles.

★ **Kimberley Walsh** was the fourth girl to make it into Girls Aloud. Her middle name is Jane and she has an older sister called Sally. Prior to auditioning for *Popstars: The Rivals*, Kimberley auditioned for *Coronation Street*. She was unsuccessful. Kimberley supports Bradford City FC and her favourite food is Thai.

★ ★ ★ ★ THE A-Z OF CELEBRITY TRIVIA ★ ★ ★ ★

★ Music manager and *X Factor* judge **Louis Walsh** made his first appearance on British television on *Popstars: The Rivals*, though he was already famous in Ireland for appearing on their edition of *Popstars*. Louis managed his first band at the age of 15. He once managed three-time *Eurovision Song Contest* winner Johnny Logan. Irish band The Revs named a song after him.

★ *My Family* mum **Zoe Wanamaker** once had a very short career as a secretary, and even toyed with the idea of becoming a nun.

★ Grammy Award-winning singer **Dionne Warwick** is the cousin of, and Aretha Franklin is the godmother of, Whitney Houston. Houston first discovered her talents singing in a gospel choir.

★ Hollywood star **Denzel Washington** has a trophy room in his California home. However, despite his two Academy Awards, Denzel doesn't have it all his own way; his wife, Pauletta, has been honoured many times as a concert pianist and her trophies adorn the room too. Before he was famous, Denzel earned $11 a day sweeping hair at a barbershop, aged 11. He said his first job prepared him for his career in acting because the best liars hang out at barbershops. He also passed up the chance to kiss Julia Roberts in *The Pelican Brief* in

★ ★ ★ ★ THE A–Z OF CELEBRITY TRIVIA ★ ★ ★ ★

1993 because he didn't want to upset his core audience of black women.

★ Pop svengali and former *Pop Idol* judge **Pete Waterman** left school illiterate – and only learned to read properly at the age of 38.

★ Comedian and presenter **Ruby Wax** script-edited for *Absolutely Fabulous*. The presenter once shared a house with Alan Rickman, when they were both struggling actors in the 80s.

★ Western icon **John Wayne** was nicknamed the Duke during his impressive career, but the real name of this macho film actor was Marion Morrison.

★ *Alien* actress **Sigourney Weaver**'s real name is Susan Weaver. She took her name from a character in the book *The Great Gatsby*, and was six foot tall by the age of 12.

★ *The Mummy* star **Rachel Weisz**'s father invented the artificial respirator and machines that sense landmines. Her mother is a psychoanalyst. Rachel drives a jaguar and is semi-fluent in German. Her last name is pronounced 'Vice'.

★ ★ ★ ★ THE A–Z OF CELEBRITY TRIVIA ★ ★ ★ ★

★ Actress and sex symbol **Raquel Welch** was considered for the role of Alexis in *Dynasty*, before Joan Collins landed the part.

★ US hip-hop star **Kanye West**'s name means 'the only one' in Swahili. He is a vocal critic of President George Bush. His mother, who was his manager earlier in his career, is a former English professor at Chicago State University.

★ Radio and television presenter **Jo Whiley** used to have a third nipple.

★ *Last King of Scotland* star **Forest Whitaker** is a trained opera singer. He once had plans to be a professional classical tenor.

★ Comedian **Paul Whitehouse** worked as a plasterer before he found fame writing for Harry Enfield's show.

★ **Pharrell Williams** – one half of uber-producers The Neptunes – has his own clothing line, BBC (Billionaire Boys Club). He has modelled for Louis Vuitton and one of his brothers is a furniture salesman in Delaware.

★ **Robbie Williams** left school at 16 and took a job as a double glazing salesman, which he absolutely hated. He wasn't very good at it either – he told customers not to buy the windows because the glazing was no good. The multi-millionaire chart-topper was voted 'Least Likely to Succeed' at school. He once posed as a beggar in New York and gave £55 to the first person to take pity on him and he claims that he will never have children because he can't bear to see them suffer. Despite not owning a driving licence, Robbie has a large collection of expensive cars, including Jaguars, Ferraris and Lamborghinis. Robbie wrote the song 'Eternity' for Geri Halliwell.

★ Actor and comedian **Robin Williams** was voted 'Least Likely to Succeed' by classmates at school.

★ In 2002, big-screen tough guy **Bruce Willis** bought 12,000 boxes of Girl Scout cookies from daughter Tallulah, then eight, to send to troops in Afghanistan. The Girl Scouts' bakery, which is only open for two months a year, had to reopen to finish the order. According to friends, Bruce had a terrible stammer as a child.

★ Beach Boys songsmith **Brian Wilson** was born deaf in one ear.

★ **Luke Wilson**, the less-famous-brother-of-Owen, was once blacklisted and banned from the *Playboy* mansion

★ ★ ★ ★ THE A-Z OF CELEBRITY TRIVIA ★ ★ ★ ★

after trying to get into a party by pretending to be his brother. He still holds the school records for the 400-metre and 800-metre athletics events for St Mark's High School in Texas.

★ Frat Pack star **Owen Wilson** shares the same middle name – Cunningham – with his brothers Luke and Andrew. The Wilson boys' father is an advertising executive and his mother is a photographer. Owen graduated from the University of Texas with an English degree. He is good friends with *Nightmare on Elm Street* director Wes Craven. The pair, along with Owen's brother Luke, once lived in the same house together. Owen owns an Australian cattle dog named Garcia.

★ Over 25 million viewers watched *Carry On* favourite **Barbara Windsor** in her first episode of *EastEnders*.

★ As a child, **Amy Winehouse** wanted to be a roller-skating waitress. Instead, she became a Grammy Award-winning singer. Perhaps unsurprisingly, tabloid regular Amy has strong opinions when it comes to cocktails. Her favourite is the Rickstasy: three parts vodka, one part Southern Comfort, one part banana liqueur and one part Bailey's. Winehouse has received attention for her distinctive style as well as her singing. Her signature beehive hairstyle has achieved praise from fashion

★ ★ ★ ★ **THE A-Z OF CELEBRITY TRIVIA** ★ ★ ★ ★

designers such as Karl Lagerfeld who likens her to Bardot. She trained at Sylvia Young Theatre School, but was apparently booted out for 'not applying herself' and for having her nose pierced. She appeared in an episode of *The Fast Show* in 1997.

★ US actress/TV host **Oprah Winfrey** should have been called Orpah, after the Biblical figure but the midwife spelled the name wrong on the birth certificate. Her production company Harpo is Oprah spelled backwards. She is a distant cousin of Elvis Presley.

★ *An Officer and a Gentleman* star **Debra Winger** was the voice of ET.

★ Journalist and presenter **Claudia Winkleman** is scared of spiders. She is not alone.

★ **Kate Winslet** gave birth to her son Joe to the music of Rufus Wainwright. The actress was bullied at school because of her weight, and nicknamed 'Blubber'. As a child, she appeared in a TV ad for Sugar Puffs cereal, and later on she starred as a patient in *Casualty*. According to Kate, her husband Sam Mendes is dead against her having plastic surgery, and might even leave her if she went ahead with it.

★ ★ ★ ★ THE A-Z OF CELEBRITY TRIVIA ★ ★ ★ ★

★ TV presenter **Dale Winton** was once a DJ on United Biscuits Industrial Radio. He is an only child.

★ At the age of seven, *Walk the Line* star **Reese Witherspoon** appeared in a television commercial for a local Nashville Florist.

★ Veteran DJ **Terry Wogan** was a virgin when he got married.

★ At the age of five, actress **Evan Rachel Wood** came very close to kissing Brad Pitt. She was flown out to LA to audition for *Interview With the Vampire*, but lost the role to Kirsten Dunst, who was 11 at the time.

★ Actor **Adam Woodyatt**, Ian Beale in *EastEnders*, was at school with cricket player and TV pundit Nasser Hussain.

★ DJ **Steve Wright** collects old radios.

★ Singer **Will Young** was a gardener before he was famous. He has a twin brother called Rupert.

★ To make ends meet in college, **Renée Zellweger** waited tables at Sugar's, a popular topless club in Texas – but she did it fully clothed. The *Bridget Jones* star has

★ ★ ★ ★ **THE A-Z OF CELEBRITY TRIVIA** ★ ★ ★ ★

two mobile phones – one for UK calls and the other for US.

★ Former *Popworld* presenter **Alex Zane** studied Medicine at University College London when he was 18. He left after a year.

★ **Catherine Zeta Jones**'s father owned a sweet factory, but the star says she rarely indulged: 'I had so many sweets and candy hanging around my house that I never even bothered with them.' Mrs Michael Douglas was once Britain's national tap-dance champion and she is also accomplished at ballet. She adores karaoke and keeps a machine in her trailer while on movie sets. When she gave birth to Dylan in 2000, the people of her hometown of Swansea, Wales, raised Welsh flags lined up to sign the town's book of congratulations, and drank champagne in her honour. Catherine's son Dylan is very close to his mother's friend George Clooney – so much so that he calls him Uncle George.

WHAT DID THEY SAY? THE A–Z OF CELEB TALK

★ ★ ★ ★ THE A–Z OF CELEB TALK ★ ★ ★ ★

★ Can you imagine Simon as a kid? His imaginary
friends probably never wanted to play with him.

> Paula Abdul on *American Idol* judge
> Simon Cowell

★ I love blinking, I do.

> Helen Adams from *Big Brother*

★ I'm not entirely dim – I knew *Gigli* was dogs★★t.

> Ben Affleck

★ I feel old when I see mousse in my opponent's hair.

> Andre Agassi

★ My grandma was like, 'Oh, Christina, you look like a
whore!' I explained that's the idea.

> Christina Aguilera

★ So, where's the Cannes Film Festival being held this year?

> Christina Aguilera

★ I was a drug dealer in Ibiza at 15. I did not excel in
drug dealing – I was terrible at it. Golden rule with
drug dealing: don't get too enthusiastic with your own
merchandise.

> Lily Allen

★ ★ ★ ★ THE A-Z OF CELEB TALK ★ ★ ★ ★

★ I think Paris [Hilton] is amazing. I mean, she's hideous, but I think she's amazing at the same time.

Lily Allen

★ If you're famous, others will give 'the famous look'. They give you that wink that says, 'Hey, we're both famous.' Ugh!

Lily Allen

★ I don't want to achieve immortality through my work; I want to achieve immortality through not dying.

Woody Allen

★ I don't think fat is pretty. If I saw some big fat leopard walking through the jungle, I'd start laughing. Or if I was at the races, I saw some 150lb greyhound running against the other lean greyhounds, I'd start laughing too. It doesn't seem very natural. It doesn't look healthy. It doesn't look sleek or stealth. It looks funny. I think that's why people through history laugh at fat people. They're round and funny-looking.

Kirstie Alley

★ I'm obsessed with crocodiles and getting eaten by one … When I hear that someone's been eaten by a crocodile or shark, I just get all gooey. I start salivating.

Tori Amos

★ ★ ★ ★ THE A-Z OF CELEB TALK ★ ★ ★ ★

★ I filled my tour manager's bed with whipped cream, yoghurt and tampons ... but I'm so un-rock n roll I even cleaned it up.

> Anastacia on the most rock'n'roll thing she's ever done

★ They have a career of their own and I'm just tagging along.

> Pamela Anderson on her breasts

★ We had back-to-back interviews, 15-minute interviews, there were about 20 of them, and to hear the people say, 'OK, we've only got ten minutes with you ... We've only got five minutes with you, we need to know this.' I said, 'You had six years to ask me questions!'

> Peter Andre on refinding fame following his stint on *I'm a Celebrity ... Get Me Out of Here!*

★ I'm pretty lazy. I do yoga every now and then, and I heard sex is a great workout.

> André 3000

★ When someone follows you all the way to the shop and watches you buy toilet roll, you know your life has changed.

> Jennifer Aniston

★ ★ ★ ★ THE A-Z OF CELEB TALK ★ ★ ★ ★

★ I've gone for each type: the rough guy; the nerdy, sweet, lovable guy; and the slick guy. I don't really have a type. Men in general are a good thing.

Jennifer Anniston

★ I think God is a giant vibrator in the sky … a pulsating force of incredible energy.

David Arquette

★ It wasn't until I got divorced that I understood the value of money.

Mel B

★ Hollywood is the only place where an amicable divorce means each person gets 50 per cent of the publicity.

Lauren Bacall

★ Any idiot can get laid when they're famous. That's easy. It's getting laid when you're not famous that takes some talent.

Kevin Bacon

★ There are two types of actors: those who say they want to be famous and those who are liars.

Kevin Bacon

★ ★ ★ ★ THE A-Z OF CELEB TALK ★ ★ ★ ★

★ One day you're filling out applications to be a waiter, and the next you're nominated for an Oscar. This business is crazy.

Alec Baldwin

★ I have been very happy, very rich, very beautiful, much adulated, very famous and very unhappy.

Brigitte Bardot on fame

★ I look at every person on this planet and realise they were all a baby at one point.

Drew Barrymore

★ Unfortunately it is true that the more flesh you show, the further up the ladder you go.

Kim Basinger

★ Charity is taking an ugly girl to lunch.

Warren Beatty

★ You've achieved success in your field when you don't know whether what you're doing is work or play.

Warren Beatty

★ My notion of a wife at forty is that a man should be able to change her, like a bank note, for two twenties.

Warren Beatty

★ ★ ★ ★ THE A-Z OF CELEB TALK ★ ★ ★ ★

★ My parents have been there for me, ever since I was about seven.

David Beckham

★ I remember so clearly us going into hospital so Victoria could have Brooklyn. I was eating a Lion bar at the time.

David Beckham

★ Alex Ferguson is the best manager I've ever had at this level. Well, he's the only manager I've actually had at this level. But he's the best manager I've ever had.

David Beckham

★ I definitely want Brooklyn to be christened, but I don't know into what religion yet.

David Beckham

★ There are so many people out there taking the p*ss out of me that if I can't take the p*ss out of myself there's something going wrong.

Victoria Beckham

★ I want a big house with a moat and dragons and a fort to keep people out!

Victoria Beckham

★ ★ ★ ★ THE A-Z OF CELEB TALK ★ ★ ★ ★

★ Everyone's showing their thong out the back of their jeans. But you shouldn't wear any. You get a better line if you wear no knickers.

Victoria Beckham

★ I am not going to be no senorita.

Victoria Beckham on moving to Spain

★ I dress sexily – but not in an obvious way. Sexy in a virginal way.

Victoria Beckham

★ If someone had told me years ago that sharing a sense of humour was so vital to partnerships, I could have avoided a lot of sex!

Kate Beckinsale

★ I have a four-year-old who's just starting to get worried about monsters, but she knows that mummy kicks monster a★★, so she's fine.

Kate Beckinsale

★ Life is a blank page. Each person holds their pen and writes their own story.

Natasha Bedingfield

★ ★ ★ ★ THE A–Z OF CELEB TALK ★ ★ ★ ★

★ I have nothing against nudity. I use my body like a dress.

Monica Bellucci

★ Charlie Chaplin used his ass better than any other actor. In all of his films his ass is practically the protagonist. For a comic, the ass has incredible importance.

Roberto Benigni

★ I carried my Oscar to bed with me. My first and only three-way happened that night.

Halle Berry

★ I spent a lot of my money on booze, birds and fast cars. The rest I just squandered.

George Best

★ Acting's a bit like sex – it's really fun to do but it's really embarrassing to talk about.

Paul Bettany

★ People think I'm some sort of strange teletubby.

Björk

★ If you have a good sex life, getting pregnant is bound to happen eventually.

Cate Blanchett

★ ★ ★ ★ THE A–Z OF CELEB TALK ★ ★ ★ ★

★ I'm not picky when it comes to food – as long as there's no meat in it.

Orlando Bloom

★ It was like kissing the Berlin wall.

Helena Bonham Carter on Woody Allen

★ If you wanted to torture me, you'd tie me down and force me to watch our first five videos.

Jon Bon Jovi

★ I wouldn't want to move to a smaller house!

Bono on why he'd never run for President

★ Pop music tells you that everything is OK and rock music tells you that it's not, but that you can change it.

Bono

★ You would think a rock star being married to a supermodel would be one of the greatest things in the world. It is.

David Bowie

★ Talking about art is like dancing about architecture.

David Bowie

★ ★ ★ ★ THE A–Z OF CELEB TALK ★ ★ ★ ★

★ Younger boyfriends? Fantastic, great. They're a little quicker taking out the garbage, that's about it.

Lara Flynn Boyle

★ If there's anything unsettling to the stomach, it's watching actors on television talk about their personal lives.

Marlon Brando

★ In this country we're just obsessed with making people celebrities before they've even done anything, which I think is just shocking.

Kelly Brook

★ Tragedy is when I cut my finger. Comedy is when you walk into an open sewer and die.

Mel Brooks

★ Don't work with children, animals or Salma Hayek. When she's on screen I may as well be flossing my teeth.

Pierce Brosnan

★ Boxing is all about getting the job done as quickly as possible, whether it takes ten or fifteen or twenty rounds.

Frank Bruno

★ Fame means when your computer modem is broken, the repair guy comes out to your house a little faster.

Sandra Bullock

★ ★ ★ ★ THE A-Z OF CELEB TALK ★ ★ ★ ★

★ Everyone told me to pass on *Speed* because it was a 'bus movie'.

Sandra Bullock

★ Once you're famous, you realise for the rest of your life, sex has to be in the bedroom.

Sandra Bullock on her pre-celebrity
sexual tryst in a taxi

★ Being a model is not as glamorous as you think. Sometimes you stand around in little clothes in the freezing weather and sometimes you burn up for hours in the sun.

Gisele Bundchen

★ My favourite review described me as the cinematic equivalent of junk mail.

Steve Buscemi

★ Acting is the shy man's revenge.

Gabriel Byrne

★ To be a good actor you have to be something like a criminal, to be willing to break the rules to strive for something new.

Nicolas Cage

★ ★ ★ ★ THE A-Z OF CELEB TALK ★ ★ ★ ★

★ Sir Laurence Olivier was full of wisdom and one day said, 'Michael, a truly great actor could step off a tall building and make himself fly like a bird.' Later he admitted he was trying to kill me.

Michael Caine

★ I never diet. I smoke. I drink now and then. I never work out. I work very hard, and I am worth every cent.

Naomi Campbell

★ I don't always wear underwear. When I'm in the heat, especially, I can't wear it. Like, if I'm wearing a flower dress, why do I have to wear underwear?

Naomi Campbell

★ I love England, especially the food – there is nothing I like more than a lovely bowl of pasta.

Naomi Campbell

★ Travelling around all the time gets a bit lonely. You just think, 'Why the hell am I doing this?' And then you look at that bank statement and you say, 'This is why I'm doing this.'

Caprice

★ ★ ★ ★ THE A–Z OF CELEB TALK ★ ★ ★ ★

★ I loved Jordan. He was one of the greatest athletes of our time.

> Mariah Carey on the death
> of the King of Jordan

★ Being chauffeured around becomes mundane. I actually hate limos. I love to drive, even though I'm not a very good driver.

> Mariah Carey

★ Whenever I watch TV and see those poor starving kids all over the world, I can't help but cry. I mean I'd love to be skinny like that but not with all those flies and death and stuff.

> Mariah Carey

★ That's the trouble with being me. At this point, nobody gives a damn what my problem is. I could literally have a tumour on the side of my head and they'd be like, 'Yeah, big deal. I'd eat a tumour every morning for the kinda money you're pulling down.'

> Jim Carrey

★ I'm finding now in my forties that the less makeup I wear, the better. I think softer is better as you get older. With everything. Except men.

> Kim Cattrall

★ ★ ★ ★ THE A-Z OF CELEB TALK ★ ★ ★ ★

★ Men cheat for the same reason that dogs lick their balls … because they can.

Kim Cattrall

★ One day there may be a wife, but for now I'm just interviewing for the position.

50 Cent

★ Everybody can be a Superman but nobody can be a Jackie Chan.

Jackie Chan

★ I think it's a mother's duty to embarrass their children.

Cher

★ I am at that age when former child stars go off the rails.

A remarkably prescient Charlotte Church

★ I was naïve in my youth.

Charlotte Church, aged 16

★ The English contribution to world cuisine – the chip.

John Cleese

★ I think pre-nups are very important. I have one and I'm not married! I have one with anyone I go to dinner with.

George Clooney

★ ★ ★ ★ THE A-Z OF CELEB TALK ★ ★ ★ ★

★ Run for office? No. I've slept with too many women, I've done too many drugs, and I've been to too many parties.

George Clooney

★ If it's illegal to rock and roll, throw my ass in jail!

Kurt Cobain

★ If you ever need anything please don't hesitate to ask someone else first.

Kurt Cobain

★ I live my life like a cool bachelor; I have a man for all occasions.

Jackie Collins

★ The problem with beauty is that it's like being born rich and getting poorer.

Joan Collins

★ You don't want to get rid of your experiences, because they're your experiences – good or bad – and you need them, but it would be great if they weren't on the video shelf.

Jennifer Connelly

★ ★ ★ ★ **THE A-Z OF CELEB TALK** ★ ★ ★ ★

★ I admit I'm being paid well, but it's no more than I deserve. After all, I've been screwed more times than a hooker.

Sean Connery

★ A word to the wise ain't necessary, it's the stupid ones who need the advice.

Bill Cosby

★ *Field of Dreams* is probably our generation's *It's A Wonderful Life*.

Kevin Costner

★ I haven't done anything particularly harsh. Harshness to me is giving somebody false hopes and not following through. That's harsh. Telling some guy or some girl who've got zero talent that they have zero talent actually is a kindness.

Simon Cowell

★ I don't think I'm too thin at all. I understand when people say, 'Well, your face gets gaunt,' but, to get your bottom half to be the right size, your face might have to be a little gaunt. You choose your battles.

Courtney Cox

★ ★ ★ ★ **THE A-Z OF CELEB TALK** ★ ★ ★ ★

★ I'd move to Los Angeles if New Zealand and Australia were swallowed up by a tidal wave, if there was a bubonic plague in England and if the continent of Africa disappeared from some Martian attack.

> Russell Crowe

★ I don't worry about image. I don't know what that is. I'm just myself.

> Tom Cruise

★ Being a Scientologist, when you drive past an accident … you know you have to do something about it because you know you're the only one that can really help.

> Tom Cruise

★ The most important lesson I've learned in this business is how to say no. I have said no to a lot of temptations, and I am glad I did.

> Penelope Cruz

★ Who the **** said that? Oh man. I want to live the life I read about. I've never even met Anna.

> Matt Damon on rumours tennis beauty
> Anna Kournikova had pole danced for him

★ ★ ★ ★ THE A-Z OF CELEB TALK ★ ★ ★ ★

★ You don't realise how useful a therapist is until you see one yourself and discover you have more problems than you ever dreamed of.

Claire Danes

★ I was at Elton John's for his birthday party. It was slightly bigger than the whole estate I grew up on.

Craig David

★ I'm a coloured, one-eyed Jew ... do I need anything else?

Sammy Davis Jr after being asked
what his handicap in golf was

★ The best thing about being a bachelor is that you can get into bed from either side.

James Dean

★ It's an absolute monster! Maybe I shouldn't have said that, how uncouth of me.

Dame Judi Dench on catching a
glimpse of 007 Daniel Craig's 'package'

★ I don't like to watch my own movies. I fall asleep in my own movies.

Robert De Niro

★ ★ ★ ★ THE A-Z OF CELEB TALK ★ ★ ★ ★

★ I'm especially scared of boogers. Snot freaks me out. If someone ever showed me a booger I'd smash their face.

Johnny Depp

★ Who cares about the story? Why do we need to learn more about the girls? Who cares about them? Don't people just want to see us in bikinis and jumping off high buildings? Hello!

Cameron Diaz

★ I grew up with a lot of boys. I probably have a lot of testosterone for a woman.

Cameron Diaz

★ When I go to restaurants, the waiters always ask me if I want a doggy bag. I'm tired of that. All you waiters, stop asking me if I want a mother★★★★★★★ doggy bag.

Snoop Dogg

★ Last Christmas I put on a Santa Claus mask, and I said to three of my ladies, 'Ho, ho, ho.' They didn't think it was funny.

Snoop Dogg

★ When I'm no longer rapping, I want to open up an ice-cream parlour and call myself Scoop Dogg.

Snoop Dogg

★ ★ ★ ★ THE A-Z OF CELEB TALK ★ ★ ★ ★

★ One minute I'm waiting for Kate to arrive to join me in the Jacuzzi for a romantic evening. The next thing I can remember is doing cold turkey in a vomit-filled cell.

Pete Doherty

★ I carry antibacterial ointment and use it after handshakes. So many people don't wash their hands after going to the bathroom that you can't be too careful.

Shannon Doherty

★ I'm allergic to drugs. They bring me out in handcuffs.

Robert Downey Jr

★ I certainly think fame is more nobly perceived if you had to fight for it. You know, if you're eating a bowl of gravel every morning and you made a guitar out of old tin pans and some cat gut.

Minnie Driver

★ I think vegetarians – for a lot of them – it's about a lack of commitment to life and relationships. There are some who just like the fact that they're controlling something in their life.

Kirsten Dunst

★ ★ ★ ★ THE A-Z OF CELEB TALK ★ ★ ★ ★

★ After a while you learn that privacy is something you can sell, but you can't buy it back.

Bob Dylan

★ People are surprised at how down-to-earth I am … I like to stay home on Friday nights and listen to *The Art of Happiness* by the Dalai Lama.

Carmen Electra

★ If I didn't have some kind of education, then I wouldn't be able to count my money.

Missy Elliot

★ Don't do drugs, don't have unprotected sex, don't be violent. Leave that to me.

Eminem

★ We don't wake up for less than $10,000.

Linda Evangelista

★ I wash once a year, whether I'm dirty or not.

Colin Farrell

★ I'm not a tortured, anger-stoked, deeply neurotic comic – just a pretty low-key normal guy. A 'hey, the glass is half-full' kind of a guy. But please keep it quiet, or I may never work again.

Will Ferrell

★ ★ ★ ★ THE A-Z OF CELEB TALK ★ ★ ★ ★

★ There's this idea that, if you're on television, you must not be a very good actress.

Calista Flockhart

★ I don't know if a country where the people are so ignorant of reality and of history, if you can call that a free world.

Jane Fonda

★ I've got ten pairs of training shoes. One for every day of the week.

Sam Fox

★ Men are very funny. If I had one of those dangly things stuffed down the front of my pants, I'd sit at home all day laughing at myself!

Dawn French

★ Television is an invention that permits you to be entertained in your living room by people you wouldn't have in your home.

David Frost

★ I was told that when you hit 40 men stop looking at you. It's true, until you slip on a mini-skirt.

Mariella Frostrup

★ ★ ★ ★ THE A-Z OF CELEB TALK ★ ★ ★ ★

★ It's about the music and that's it. I'm not an entertainer. But I do entertain people, see what I mean.

Liam Gallagher

★ Everyone knows that, if you've got a brother, you're going to fight.

Liam Gallagher

★ Sure, I love Liam, but not as much as I love Pot Noodles.

Noel Gallagher on his brother

★ I know I've got Irish blood because I wake up every day with a hangover.

Noel Gallagher

★ We have devalued the idea of marriage as a legal contract. When we think of marriage now, we think too much of the day, the dress and the drunk uncle.

Bob Geldof

★ I hate ridiculous names; my weird name has haunted me all my life.

Peaches Geldof

★ It makes me think of women who don't shave their legs.

Sarah Michelle Gellar on feminism

★ ★ ★ ★ THE A-Z OF CELEB TALK ★ ★ ★ ★

★ I've got an in-built, maybe magnetic, natural, animal-magnetic navigation system.

Uri Gellar

★ I've spent a lot of time asking my wife what women want from their husbands, and as far as I can make out its somewhere between conversation and chocolate.

Mel Gibson

★ Whenever women are together for more than two days they talk about their periods.

Whoopi Goldberg

★ He's claiming abuse. I pay my wife good money for a little abuse; a good spanking sometimes. I don't know what he's complaining about.

Cuba Gooding Jr on David Gest's lawsuit against Liza Minnelli for physical abuse

★ Life is a journey I don't have a map for.

Delta Goodrem

★ The things I know make sense.

Jade Goody

★ Where's East Angular [sic] though? I thought that was abroad.

Jade Goody

★ ★ ★ ★ THE A-Z OF CELEB TALK ★ ★ ★ ★

★ They were trying to use me as an escape goat.

Jade Goody

★ Very big-mouthed! Literally, physically, she has a very big mouth. When I was kissing her I was aware of a faint echo.

Hugh Grant on Julia Roberts

★ I had a huge crush on Olga Korbut, the gymnast. The only other person was Cliff Richard, which is embarrassing – it means that when I was seven I had bad taste and was presumably gay.

Hugh Grant

★ With two movies opening this summer, I have no relaxing time at all. Whatever I have is spent in a drunken stupor.

Hugh Grant

★ I'm really demanding. No girl really wants just a guy. You want a prince. You want Jesus. So when he comes around and his name is like Steve, what are you supposed to do?

Macy Gray

★ My mother said it was simple to keep a man, you must be a maid in the living room, a cook in the kitchen and a whore in the bedroom. I said I'd hire the other two and take care of the bedroom bit.

Jerry Hall

★ ★ ★ ★ THE A-Z OF CELEB TALK ★ ★ ★ ★

★ I must say that I do wrestle with the amount of money I make, but at the end of the day what am I gonna say? I took less money so Rupert Murdoch could have more?

Tom Hanks

★ There are many dying children out there whose last wish is to meet me.

David Hasselhoff

★ I've got taste. It's inbred in me.

David Hasselhoff

★ There are only three ages for women in Hollywood – Babe, District Attorney and Driving Miss Daisy.

Goldie Hawn

★ I want to be a WAG.

Chanelle Hayes

★ Picasso had his pink period and his blue period. I am in my blonde period right now.

Hugh Hefner

★ It's funny how most people love the dead. Once you're dead you're made for life.

Jimi Hendrix

★ ★ ★ ★ THE A-Z OF CELEB TALK ★ ★ ★ ★

★ If you want to sacrifice the admiration of many men for the criticism of one, go ahead, get married.

Katharine Hepburn

★ I just accepted them as a great accessory to every outfit.

Jennifer Love Hewitt on her breasts

★ I don't want to ever, ever do something in life that isn't fun. Ever.

Jennifer Love Hewitt

★ I'll phone up and say, 'Hi, it's Paris Hilton,' and they'll say, 'Yes this is the Paris Hilton.' So I'm like, 'Yes, I know, I'm Paris Hilton.' It can go on for hours like some bad comedy film.

Paris Hilton on booking a room in the hotel of the same name

★ Kabbalah helps you confront your fears. Like if a girl borrowed my clothes and never gave them back, and I saw her wearing them months later, I would confront her.

Paris Hilton

★ Every woman should have four pets in her life. A mink in her closet, a jaguar in her garage, a tiger in her bed and a jackass who pays for everything.

Paris Hilton

★ ★ ★ ★ THE A-Z OF CELEB TALK ★ ★ ★ ★

★ What's Walmart, do they sell like wall stuff?
    Paris Hilton on the American supermarket chain

★ If I could read a book, I'd definitely read one of yours.
    Paris Hilton

★ I knew I'd end up marrying Tom [Cruise] at some point. My medium said that years ago.
    Katie Holmes

★ Eleventy-twelve pence? I don't get it. How much is that then?
    Chantelle Houghton

★ People are often jealous of my looks but that's their problem not mine.
    Chantelle Houghton

★ I'm superstitious ... but not like wear the same underwear for two weeks superstitious.
    Kate Hudson

★ Nothing irritates me more than chronic laziness in others. Mind you, it's only mental sloth I object to. Physical sloth can be heavenly.
    Elizabeth Hurley

★ ★ ★ ★ THE A–Z OF CELEB TALK ★ ★ ★ ★

★ Up until they go to school, they're relatively portable.

Elizabeth Hurley on children

★ Love is like wine. To sip is fine, but to empty the bottle is a headache.

Julio Iglesias

★ Crikey, mate. You're far safer dealing with crocodiles and western diamondback rattlesnakes than the executives and the producers and all those sharks in the big MGM building.

Steve Irwin

★ They gave me a nutritionist. They figured that, since I was Australian, I'd think dieting was having six beers a day instead of ten.

Hugh Jackman on his Hollywood producers

★ I can't believe people got so upset at the sight of a single breast! America is so parochial, I may just have to move to Europe where people are more mature about things like that!

Janet Jackson on *that* Super Bowl performance

★ Me and Janet really are two different people.

Michael Jackson

★ ★ ★ ★ THE A-Z OF CELEB TALK ★ ★ ★ ★

★ The golf course is the only place I can go dressed like a pimp and fit in perfectly. Anywhere else, lime-green pants and alligator shoes, I got a cop on my ass.

Samuel L Jackson

★ I think everyone who says they don't like watching themselves in movies should stop lying.

Samuel L Jackson

★ I'd rather be dead than singing 'Satisfaction' at 45.

Mick Jagger in 1975

★ You know, obviously, I have this sort of strange animal magnetism. It's very hard for me to take my eyes off myself.

Mick Jagger

★ There are no playboys any more. I've always been a career-minded person. Any vague resemblance of my life to a playboy's is purely coincidental.

Mick Jagger

★ When I realised Beyonce mimes half or three-quarters of her show, that took a lot away for me. I thought, 'Are you an artist or are you an actress?'

Jamelia

★ ★ ★ ★ THE A-Z OF CELEB TALK ★ ★ ★ ★

★ I definitely believe in plastic surgery. I don't want to be an old hag. There's no fun in that.

Scarlett Johansson

★ People think I'm some brazen harlot, but I'm not out there with every Tom, Dick and Harry or catching hepatitis

Scarlett Johansson

★ Madonna, best f***ing live act? F**k off! Since when has lip synching been live? Anyone who lip synchs in public on stage when you've paid £75 to see them should be shot. That's me off her Christmas card list, but do I give a toss? NO!

Elton John

★ Oh, God, I struggle with low self-esteem all the time. I think everyone does. I have so much wrong with me, it's unbelievable!

Angelina Jolie

★ An Oscar is nice, but I never take that seriously and I make a point never to see awards. I give them away immediately, so that they are never in my environment.

Angelina Jolie

★ ★ ★ ★ THE A-Z OF CELEB TALK ★ ★ ★ ★

★ I'm not sure if there was a key event that changed me, but I first had sex when I was 14.

Angelina Jolie

★ Some people may be famous for creating a pencil sharpener. I'm famous for my tits.

Jordan

★ I want to look a bit covered-up and virginal. Pete knows what's underneath, I suppose, but then again so does everyone else.

Jordan on her wedding

★ In my films my breasts are definitely computer animated, because I don't have any. They spend most of the money in the film's budget just making my breasts. That's why producers never like me.

Milla Jovovich

★ You can get Indian food at three in the morning, but I personally don't want Indian food at three in the morning. I want to go for a walk in my nightgown!

Ashley Judd on the pros and cons of living in New York

★ Just the other day I sent the girlfriend a huge pile of snow … I rang her up and said, 'Did you get my drift?'

Peter Kay

★ ★ ★ ★ THE A–Z OF CELEB TALK ★ ★ ★ ★

★ My talent has overwhelmed me – it automatically beats the pen and pad to the punch. Lyrics come just like that, out of nowhere. God blessed me with a talent I don't see anybody else with.

R Kelly

★ All of a sudden you're like the Bin Laden of America. Osama Bin Laden is the only one who knows what I'm going through.

R Kelly

★ If I want to be alone, some place I can write, I can read, I can pray, I can cry, I can do whatever I want – I go to the bathroom.

Alicia Keys

★ I've been in the closet with it for a while. I don't know, guess I would have to say I'm the rookie of the year.

K-Fed

★ My album is sure to set the dance floors across the world on fire!

K-Fed

★ Well, I can wear heels now.

Nicole Kidman on life after Tom Cruise

★ ★ ★ ★ THE A-Z OF CELEB TALK ★ ★ ★ ★

★ What's the point of doing something good if nobody's watching?

> Nicole Kidman

★ Hook me up with a great photographer, a clever stylist and an expert retoucher, and together we create a beautiful illusion.

> Heidi Klum

★ For five minutes it's fantastic, but oxygen deprivation is a big problem.

> Keira Knightly on wearing
> a corset for a role

★ Officially, I am not a woman any more. Dublin has turned me into a man.

> Keira Knightley on drinking with the boys
> while she filmed *King Arthur* in the Irish capital

★ People look at us head to toe, judge us and think we're not human. We are. Nobody's a celebrity but God.

> Beyonce Knowles

★ Boyfriends have to understand my needs. I shower four times a day.

> Anna Kournikova

★ ★ ★ ★ THE A-Z OF CELEB TALK ★ ★ ★ ★

★ In college I castrated 21 rats, and I got pretty good at it.

Lisa Kudrow

★ It's a way to keep things in perspective. Acting can be so much fun that it's easy to forget that what you're doing is a job. But, if I've got my tie on, I'm going to work.

Ashton Kutcher, explaining why he wore a tie to work on the set of *That '70s Show*

★ You can never be overdressed. If somebody says you're overdressed, they're underdressed.

Ashton Kutcher

★ I tried not wearing underwear for a while. Bad move.

Ashton Kutcher

★ I always feel like I'm the butler when I'm with famous people.

Ashton Kutcher

★ School teaches you what to do with the rest of your life. I already knew.

Avril Lavigne

★ I rejected some gorgeous publicity shots because they just didn't look like me. I won't wear skanky clothes

★ ★ ★ ★ THE A-Z OF CELEB TALK ★ ★ ★ ★

that show off my booty, my belly or boobs. I have a great body. I could be Britney. I could be better than Britney.

Avril Lavigne

★ I'm kind of ashamed to be a celebrity. I don't understand wanting to read about other people's dirty laundry. I think celebrity is the biggest red herring society has ever pulled on itself.`

Jude Law

★ I'm rather more Marilyn Manson than Marilyn Monroe.

Nigella Lawson

★ We want to be the band to dance to when the bomb drops.

Simon Le Bon

★ I only do this because I'm having fun. The day I stop having fun, I'll just walk away. I wasn't going to have fun doing a teen movie again. I don't want to do this for the rest of my life. I don't want to spend the rest of my youth doing this in this industry. There's so much I want to discover.

Heath Ledger

★ ★ ★ ★ THE A–Z OF CELEB TALK ★ ★ ★ ★

★ Notice that the stiffest tree is most easily cracked, while the bamboo or willow survives by bending with the wind.

Bruce Lee

★ Charlton Heston admitted he had a drinking problem, and I said to myself, 'Thank God this guy doesn't own any guns!'

David Letterman

★ I'm five friggin' three! People keep saying I'm five one.

Lucy Liu

★ From an early age I was aware of what America meant, and how the Marines at Camp Pendleton were ready to defend us at a moment's notice. I also remember what fabulous bodies those troops had.

Heather Locklear

★ I'm not very politically involved. And I don't like to talk about it. I mean, if you say you're a Democrat, that'll turn off Republicans and that's half your fan base.

Lindsay Lohan

★ I guess if the tabloids are going to bring attention to me, they might as well bring it to my boobs.

Lindsay Lohan

★ ★ ★ ★ THE A-Z OF CELEB TALK ★ ★ ★ ★

★ I had no idea who he was but I remember him saying he was a successful actor.

> Lindsay Lohan on an economical-
> with-the-truth Calum Best

★ It's a shame to call somebody a 'diva' simply because they work harder than everybody else.

> Jennifer Lopez

★ All I can say is, if they show my butt in a movie, it better be a wide shot.

> Jennifer Lopez

★ He's the kind of guy that would be really sweet to a girl and bring her flowers, but still take a pee in the alley.

> Traci Lords on Johnny Depp

★ In rock, you are nothing until you've slept with Winona Ryder and had a feud with me.

> Courtney Love

★ I don't mean to be a diva, but some days you wake up and you're Barbra Streisand.

> Courtney Love

★ ★ ★ ★ THE A-Z OF CELEB TALK ★ ★ ★ ★

★ I curse like a sailor, I show my boobs, I'm a rock star and I smoke like hell.

Courtney Love

★ I used to do drugs, but don't tell anyone or it will ruin my image.

Courtney Love

★ Television has no regard for the absence of talent … it merely makes you famous.

Joanna Lumley

★ Listen, everyone is entitled to my opinion.

Madonna

★ I have the same goal I've had ever since I was a girl. I want to rule the world.

Madonna

★ I saw losing my virginity as a career move.

Madonna

★ I think that everyone should get married at least once, so you can see what a silly, outdated institution it is.

Madonna

★ ★ ★ ★ THE A-Z OF CELEB TALK ★ ★ ★ ★

★ When I get down on my knees, it is not to pray.

Madonna

★ I miss New York. I still love how people talk to you on the street – just assault you and tell you what they think of your jacket.

Madonna

★ He [Tom Cruise] is a good person. I think he gets a raw deal, just as I think the orphans in Malawi get a raw deal; just as I think a lot of marginalised people get a raw deal.

Madonna

★ You have to be around people that are interested in having strange times. That doesn't always have to be depraved sex orgies, of course – it can be conservative sex orgies.

Marilyn Manson

★ I say no to drugs, but they don't listen.

Marilyn Manson

★ It's tiny, what can I do?

Ricky Martin on his bum

★ ★ ★ ★ THE A-Z OF CELEB TALK ★ ★ ★ ★

★ Sex is one of the most wholesome, beautiful and natural experiences that money can buy.

Steve Martin.

★ Being naked on set is like swimming naked – it makes you feel powerful.

Ewan McGregor

★ We asked an ex-SAS man where the most dangerous place was that we would be visiting and he pointed to the United States.

Ewan McGregor on his round-the-world
bike documentary

★ If you want to get the girl, tell them you're gay. That's my advice.

Sir Ian McKellen

★ The whole business is built on ego, vanity, self-satisfaction, and it's total crap to pretend it's not.

George Michael

★ At the studio she said hello to everybody but me. She thought I was there just to make the drinks.

Christina Milian on Jennifer Lopez

★ ★ ★ ★ THE A-Z OF CELEB TALK ★ ★ ★ ★

★ Smoking is one of the leading causes of all statistics.

Liza Minnelli

★ It was no great tragedy being Judy Garland's daughter. I had tremendously interesting childhood years – except they had little to do with being a child.

Liza Minnelli

★ I don't try to be a sex bomb. I am one.

Kylie Minogue

★ Hollywood is a place where they'll pay you a thousand dollars for a kiss and fifty cents for your soul.

Marilyn Monroe

★ A career is born in public – talent in privacy.

Marilyn Monroe

★ Three things have helped me successfully go through the ordeals of life: an understanding husband, a good analyst and millions of dollars.

Mary Tyler Moore

★ I enjoy being a highly overpaid actor.

Roger Moore

★ ★ ★ ★ THE A-Z OF CELEB TALK ★ ★ ★ ★

★ I'm not used to the C word. That is sort of a new deal. It is so funny. C'mon, I was not raised to take myself that seriously.

> Brittany Murphy is still not used
> to being a celebrity

★ If you're playing a poker game and you look around the table and can't tell who the sucker is, it's you.

> Paul Newman

★ Adultery? Why fool about with hamburger when you can have steak at home.

> Paul Newman

★ You only lie to two people in your life: your girlfriend and the police.

> Jack Nicholson

★ I only take Viagra when I am with more than one woman.

> Jack Nicholson

★ My mother never saw the irony in calling me a son-of-a-bitch.

> Jack Nicholson

★ ★ ★ ★ THE A-Z OF CELEB TALK ★ ★ ★ ★

★ What is a younger woman? I'm pretty old, so almost every woman is younger than me.

Jack Nicholson

★ Men are like steel. When they lose their temper they lose their worth.

Chuck Norris

★ I don't think I've got bad taste. I've got no taste.

Graham Norton

★ I've seen a toddler eat her way through a pound in weight of sweets. She might as well have done an Ecstasy tablet.

Jamie Oliver

★ If I had a drug addiction, I would be in a thingy – like Promises, the Malibu [rehabilitation] place. You don't see me there. So, like, come on. It's crazy.

Mary-Kate Olsen

★ I don't think there's anything sexy about looking like you've just come out of Auschwitz.

Kelly Osbourne on size zero

★ I bit the head off a live bat the other night. It was like eating a Crunchie wrapped in chamois leather.

Ozzy Osbourne

★ ★ ★ ★ THE A-Z OF CELEB TALK ★ ★ ★ ★

★ To be Ozzy Osbourne, it's not so bad. It could be worse. I could be Sting.

Ozzy Osbourne

★ I can honestly say all the bad things that ever happened to me were directly attributed to drugs and alcohol. I mean, I would never urinate at the Alamo at nine o'clock in the morning dressed in a woman's evening dress sober.

Ozzy Osbourne

★ There's nothing like an English weirdo. We come up with the best nutters of any country.

Sharon Osbourne

★ I remember when I was seven, sitting backstage in Vegas while these topless showgirls adjusted their G-strings in front of me. It was a strange way to grow up.

Donny Osmond

★ We have the power to make things cool, hot, and sexy – from the clothes we wear to the cars we drive to the bling we buy. Now we are going to make voting cool. We are the true leaders of today.

P Diddy

★ ★ ★ ★ THE A–Z OF CELEB TALK ★ ★ ★ ★

★ I was the first woman to burn my bra – it took the fire department four days to put it out.

Dolly Parton

★ People always ask me how long it takes to do my hair. I don't know, I'm never there.

Dolly Parton

★ Plastic surgeons are always making mountains out of molehills.

Dolly Parton

★ I have got little feet because nothing grows in the shade.

Dolly Parton

★ I think it is so sad that I am in a movie with all these gorgeous actresses and that my nude scene is with Bruce Willis.

Matthew Perry on his role in
The Whole Ten Yards

★ Just standing around looking beautiful is so boring.

Michelle Pfeiffer

★ We're just going to do the best we can, hold our breath and hope we've set enough money aside for their therapy.

Michelle Pfeiffer on her children

★ ★ ★ ★ THE A-Z OF CELEB TALK ★ ★ ★ ★

★ I change my mind so much I need two boyfriends and a girlfriend.

Pink

★ The more things you own, the more people you need to employ.

Billie Piper

★ It makes you feel permanently like a girl walking past construction workers.

Brad Pitt on fame

★ Reporters ask me what I feel China should do about Tibet. Who cares what I think China should do? I'm a f**king actor! I'm here for entertainment. Basically, when you whittle everything away, I'm a grown man who puts on makeup.

Brad Pitt

★ I'm one of those people you hate because of genetics.

Brad Pitt

★ You can call me Jimmy or you can call me Iggy. My parents called me James Osterberg, Jr. Iggy was a nickname hung on me that I didn't particularly like.

Iggy Pop

★ ★ ★ ★ THE A-Z OF CELEB TALK ★ ★ ★ ★

★ Prince Charles asked me if I was in the original *Star Wars*. I was like, 'What are you smoking?'

Natalie Portman

★ Truth is like the sun. You can shut it out for a time, but it ain't goin' away.

Elvis Presley

★ The place is so plastic. I would have felt more at home if I'd covered myself in clingfilm.

Gordon Ramsay on LA

★ Health food may be good for the conscience but Oreos taste a hell of a lot better.

Robert Redford

★ I'm a meathead. I can't help it, man. You've got smart people and you've got dumb people.

Keanu Reeves

★ The media is obsessed with who I'm going to date next. It puts a lot of pressure on me. If I got as much action as they say, wow, I'd be having a lot of fun.

Tara Reid

★ I certainly hope I'm not still answering child-star questions by the time I reach menopause.

Christina Ricci

★ ★ ★ ★ THE A–Z OF CELEB TALK ★ ★ ★ ★

★ If I'm in the middle of hitting a most fantastic cross-court backhand top spin and someone says, 'Can you stop now and have sex?' I'll say, 'No thanks!'

Cliff Richard

★ Doing love scenes is always awkward. I mean, it's just not a normal thing to go to work and lie in bed with your co-worker.

Denise Richards

★ Passing the vodka bottle. And playing the guitar.

Keith Richards on keeping fit at his age

★ I've never had a problem with drugs. I've had problems with the police.

Keith Richards

★ We are not that flash, me or the missus [Madonna]. In fact, we are quite low-maintenance.

Guy Ritchie

★ I wouldn't do nudity in films. For me, personally, to act with my clothes on is a performance; to act with my clothes off is a documentary.

Julia Roberts

★ ★ ★ ★ **THE A-Z OF CELEB TALK** ★ ★ ★ ★

★ Halle Berry doesn't know it yet, but we'll be doing a romantic comedy soon. You see, The Rock has the same kind of fantasies as everyone else.

The Rock

★ You know the world is going crazy when the best rapper is a white guy, the best golfer is a black guy, the tallest guy in the NBA is Chinese, the Swiss hold the America's Cup, France is accusing the US of arrogance, Germany doesn't want to go to war, and the three most powerful men in America are named 'Bush', 'Dick' and 'Colon'.

Chris Rock

★ I feel my best when I'm happy.

Winona Ryder

★ It's hard to be naked and not be upstaged by your nipples.

Susan Sarandon

★ I've looked in the mirror every day for 20 years. It's the same face.

Claudia Schiffer

★ I think that gay marriage is something that should be between a man and a woman.

Arnold Schwarzenegger

★ ★ ★ ★ THE A-Z OF CELEB TALK ★ ★ ★ ★

★ I have a love interest in every one of my films – a gun.

Arnold Schwarzenegger

★ Instead of getting married again, I'm going to find a woman I don't like and just give her a house.

Steven Seagal

★ Why is there only one Monopolies Commission?

Jerry Seinfeld

★ He said, 'I want you to play an alcoholic, drug-addicted pornographer.' And I said, 'I've been rehearsing for this part for 20 years.'

Charlie Sheen

★ Smoking kills. If you're killed, you've lost a very important part of your life.

Brooke Shields

★ I think that the film *Clueless* was very deep. I think it was deep in the way that it was very light. I think lightness has to come from a very deep place if it's true lightness.

Alicia Silverstone

★★★★ THE A-Z OF cELEB TALK ★★★★

★ I'm going to let my real talent show, not just stand there and dance around. Personally, I'd never lip-synch. It's just not me.

> Ashlee Simpson prior to getting caught
> lip-synching on American television

★ I want to be a diva, like 'people-totally-respect-my-music' diva, not diva like 'carry-my-diet-Coke-around'.

> Jessica Simpson

★ Musically, my dream is to do what Norah Jones did. I can't play the piano, but to sit next to it and just sing.

> Jessica Simpson

★ Is this chicken or is this fish? I know it's tuna but it says chicken by the sea.

> Jessica Simpson

★ I'm not anorexic. I'm from Texas. Are there people from Texas that are anorexic? I've never heard of one. And that includes me.

> Jessica Simpson

★ Alcohol may be man's worst enemy, but the Bible says love your enemy.

> Frank Sinatra

★ ★ ★ ★ THE A-Z OF CELEB TALK ★ ★ ★ ★

★ People always ask me, did I ever learn anything when I was a stripper? Yeah, I did. One man plus two beers equals 20 dollars.

Anna Nicole Smith

★ I don't have a boyfriend right now. I'm looking for anyone with a job that I don't have to support.

Anna Nicole Smith

★ If you haven't turned rebel by 20, you've got no heart; if you haven't turned establishment by 30, you've got no brains!

Kevin Spacey

★ The cool thing about being famous is travelling. I have always wanted to travel across seas, like to Canada and stuff.

Britney Spears

★ Where the hell is Australia anyway?

Britney Spears

★ I always listen to 'N Sync's 'Tearin' Up My Heart'. It reminds me to wear a bra.

Britney Spears

★ ★ ★ ★ THE A-Z OF CELEB TALK ★ ★ ★ ★

★ I like most of the places I've been to, but I've never really wanted to go to Japan, simply because I don't like eating fish, and I know that's very popular out there in Africa.

Britney Spears

★ I would rather start out somewhere small, like London or England.

Britney Spears on treading the boards

★ The movies are weird. You actually have to think about them when you watch them.

Britney Spears on the
Sundance Film Festival

★ The only happy artist is a dead artist, because only then you can't change. After I die, I'll probably come back as a paintbrush.

Sylvester Stallone

★ Sometimes you have to sacrifice your performance for high heels.

Gwen Stefani

★ All musicians are fun to get drunk with, except the ones who are cleaning up their act. We steer clear of those.

Rod Stewart

★ ★ ★ ★ THE A-Z OF CELEB TALK ★ ★ ★ ★

★ I believe in the theory that anyone can get laid. It's just a matter of lowering your standards enough.

Michael Stipe

★ It's better to smoke rollies than straights because straights have chemicals that keep them burning. So if you have to really smoke, smoke rollies.

Joss Stone when being asked for a health tip at a US National Heart, Lung And Blood Institute fundraiser

★ I'm very old-fashioned. Occasionally I do wear underwear.

Sharon Stone

★ I can't put a sentence together – thank God I can take my clothes off.

Sharon Stone

★ My biggest nightmare is I'm driving home and get sick and go to hospital. I say, 'Please help me.' And the people say, 'Hey, you look like …' And I'm dying while they're wondering whether I'm Barbra Streisand.

Barbra Streisand

★ I just don't like the idea of her singing my songs. Who the hell does she thinks she is? The world doesn't need another Streisand!

Barbra Streisand on Diana Ross

★ ★ ★ ★ THE A-Z OF CELEB TALK ★ ★ ★ ★

★ I've got a phone, answer machine, TV set, computer, hand grenade — everything you need to run a business in Los Angeles.

Ice T

★ I believe in the Golden Rule — The Man with the Gold ... Rules.

Mr T

★ People ask me if I went to film school. And I tell them, 'No, I went to films.'

Quentin Tarantino

★ I, along with the critics, have never taken myself very seriously.

Elizabeth Taylor

★ Big girls need big diamonds.

Elizabeth Taylor

★ It is better to have a relationship with someone who cheats on you than with someone who does not flush the toilet.

Uma Thurman

★ ★ ★ ★ THE A-Z OF CELEB TALK ★ ★ ★ ★

★ This is only my first record so you guys stick with me –
we've got depression and drug addiction to go through.

Justin Timberlake

★ I kiss people with my soul. I don't kiss them with my
mouth.

Justin Timberlake

★ For me, math is in the music. If you can make math
come alive and get students really excited about math,
then they will gain a true understanding of math and
its many uses.

Justin Timberlake

★ In three movies I was overweight. And they all made
100 million, so I knew people weren't coming to see
my body.

John Travolta

★ Don't judge someone until they have tossed your salad.

John Travolta

★ I know there are nights when I have power, when I
could put on something and walk in somewhere and,
if there is a man who doesn't look at me, it's because
he's gay.

Kathleen Turner

★ ★ ★ ★ THE A-Z OF CELEB TALK ★ ★ ★ ★

★ I'd never call up a restaurant and say, 'Hi, I'm Shania Twain, and I want your best table.' But I let my friends and family do it.

Shania Twain

★ You have no idea how expensive it is to look this cheap.

Steven Tyler

★ When I was in prison, I was wrapped up in all those deep books. That Tolstoy crap – people shouldn't read that stuff.

Mike Tyson

★ If you could put the career of Will Smith, Sean 'Puffy' Combs, LA Reid and Michael Jackson all in one, there you have it. Those are some big shoes to fill, but I've got big feet.

Usher

★ I am the Fred Astaire of karate.

Jean-Claude Van Damme

★ All Britain cares about is publicity. That's why you're going to negotiate with those weak-ass terrorists. You can't negotiate, that means they've won. We are the protectors, the superpower, and we will win.

Vanilla Ice on Iraq

★ ★ ★ ★ THE A-Z OF CELEB TALK ★ ★ ★ ★

★ These are two consonants and a vowel I'm very proud of.

Carol Vorderman on being awarded an MBE

★ That's one of the weird things about celebrity is that you don't know who's watching ... It's my least favourite part of acting – celebrity.

Denzel Washington

★ I don't feel we did wrong in taking this great country away from them. There were great numbers of people who needed new land, and the Indians were selfishly trying to keep it for themselves.

John Wayne

★ People find out I'm an actress and I see that 'whore' look flicker across their eyes.

Rachel Weisz

★ Behind every successful man is a woman holding a brush and shovel cleaning up the sh★t he's too full of himself to notice.

Raquel Welch

★ I want to be like David Bowie or Iggy Pop and I'm more like Norman Wisdom.

Robbie Williams

★ ★ ★ ★ THE A-Z OF CELEB TALK ★ ★ ★ ★

★ Ah, yes, divorce, from the Latin word meaning to rip out a man's genitals through his wallet.

Robin Williams

★ On the one hand, we'll never experience childbirth. On the other hand, we can open all our own jars.

Bruce Willis on women

★ I've always had confidence. Before I was famous, that confidence got me into trouble. After I got famous, it just got me into more trouble.

Bruce Willis

★ The [kissing] scene with Carmen Electra and Amy Smart ended up being very challenging for me. I wanted to make sure we got it right, so there were a lot of takes, a lot of rehearsals. I showed up early that day!

Owen Wilson

★ Most people my age spend a lot of time thinking about what they're going to do for the next five or ten years. The time they spend thinking about their life, I just spend drinking.

Amy Winehouse

★ ★ ★ ★ THE A-Z OF CELEB TALK ★ ★ ★ ★

★ By the time you've had two of them, you're like, don't even try and go anywhere. Sit down and stay down, until the birds start singing.

> Amy Winehouse on her favourite
> cocktail Rickstasy

★ I'm either a really good drunk or I'm an out-and-out sh★t, horrible, violent, abusive, emotional drunk.

> Amy Winehouse

★ All my life I have always known I was born to greatness.

> Oprah Winfrey

★ It's getting harder for directors to cast women to play 60-year-olds because they all look 40.

> Kate Winslet

★ Everyone in Hollywood is either not drinking alcohol because of their diet, or is a reformed alcoholic, or is in rehab. Hollywood is just so boring.

> Catherine Zeta Jones pines for the valleys

★ A million pounds is not a lot of money.

> Catherine Zeta Jones

My Name Is....
Real Names Of
The Stars

★ ★ ★ ★ REAL NAMES OF THE STARS ★ ★ ★ ★

A

Aaliyah	Aaliyah Dana Haughton
Russ Abbot	Russell Roberts
Ben Affleck	Benjamin Geza Affleck
Clay Aiken	Clayton Holmes Grissom
Alan Alda	Alphonso D'Abruzzo
Akon	Aliaune Damala Bouga Time Puru Nacka Lu Lu Lu Badara Akon Thiam
Fred Allen	John Sullivan
Woody Allen	Allen Konigsberg
Tori Amos	Myra Ellen Amos
Trey Anastasio	Ernest Joseph Anastasio III
Julie Andrews	Julia Wells
Jennifer Aniston	Jennifer Anastassakis
Adam Ant	Stuart Leslie Goddard
Little Anthony	Anthony Gourdine
Marc Anthony	Marco Antonio Muniz
Laura Antonelli	Laura Antonaz
apl.de.ap	Allan Pineda Lindo
Fiona Apple	Fiona Apple McAfee Maggart
Eve Arden	Eunice Quedens
Beatrice Arthur	Bernice Frankel
Jean Arthur	Gladys Greene
Ashanti	Ashanti Shaquoya 'Shani Bani' Douglas

★ ★ ★ ★ REAL NAMES OF THE STARS ★ ★ ★ ★

Fred Astaire	Frederick Austerlitz
Frankie Avalon	Francis Thomas Avalonne

B

Babyface	Kenneth Brian Edmonds
Lauren Bacall	Betty Joan Perske
Erykah Badu	Erica Wright
Cheryl Baker	Rita Crudgington
Ginger Baker	Peter Edward Baker
LaVern Baker	Delores Williams
Afrika Bambaataa	Kevin Donovan
Eric Bana	Eric Banadinovic
Anne Bancroft	Anna-Maria Louisa Italiano
Antonio Banderas	José Antonio Dominguez Bandera
Brigitte Bardot	Camille Javal
Syd Barrett	Roger Keith Barrett
Rona Barrett	Rona Burstein
Gene Barry	Eugene Klass
John Barrymore	John Blythe
Michael Barrymore	Michael Parker
Ol' Dirty Bastard	Russell Tyrone Jones
Beck	Bek David Campbell
Jeff Beck	Geoffery Arnold Beck
Captain Beefheart	Don Van Vliet
Harry Belafonte	Harold George Belafonte

★ ★ ★ ★ REAL NAMES OF THE STARS ★ ★ ★ ★

Tony Bennett	Anthony Dominick Benedetto
Tom Berenger	Thomas Michael Moore
Beyonce	Beyonce Giselle Knowles
Bez	Mark Berry
Jello Biafra	Eric Reed Boucher
Bo Bice	Harold Elwin Bice, III
Big Daddy	Shirley Crabtree
Björk	Björk Gudmundsdottir
Cilla Black	Priscilla White
Jack Black	Thomas Black, Jr
Big Boi	Antwan André Patton
Marc Bolan	Marc Feld
Michael Bolton	Michael Bolotin
Bizzy Bone	Bryon Anthony McCane II
The Big Bopper	Jiles Perry Richardson
Gary U.S. Bonds	Gary Anderson
Jon Bon Jovi	John Francis Bongiovi Jr.
Bono	Paul David Hewson
Sonny Bono	Salvatore Philip Bono
Pat Boone	Charles Eugene Boone
David Bowie	David Robert Jones
Big Bad Brad (Linkin Park)	Bradford Phillip Delson
Michelle Branch	Michelle Jacquet DeSevren Branch-Landau
Marlon Brando	Marlon Junior Brandeau

★ ★ ★ ★ REAL NAMES OF THE STARS ★ ★ ★ ★

Fanny Brice	Fanny Borach
Jeff Bridges	Jeffrey Leon Bridges
Charles Bronson	Charles Buchinski
Mel Brooks	Mel Kaminsky
Jackson Browne	Clyde Jackson Browne
Yul Brynner	Yul Taidje Kahn, Jr
Buckethead	Brian Carroll
Chris de Burgh	Christopher John de Burgh
Davison	
George Burns	Nathan Birnbaum
Ellen Burstyn	Edna Gilhooley
Richard Burton	Richard Walter Jenkins

C

Vitamin C	Colleen Fitzpatrick
James Caan	James Langston Edmund Caan
Nicolas Cage	Nicholas Kim Coppola
Michael Caine	Maurice Micklewhite
Randy California	Randy Craig Wolfe
Irene Cara	Irene Escalera
Eric Carr	Paul Charles Caravello
50 Cent	Curtis Jackson
Gene Chandler	Eugene Dixon
Cyd Charisse	Tula Ellice Finklea
Ray Charles	Ray Charles Robinson
Chubby Checker	Ernest Evans

★ ★ ★ ★ REAL NAMES OF THE STARS ★ ★ ★ ★

Cher	Cherilyn Sarkisian La Piere
Lou Christie	Lugee Alfredo Giovanni Sacco
Charlotte Church	Charlotte Maria Reed
Gene Clark	Harold Eugene Clark
John Cleese	John Cheese
Patsy Cline	Virginia Patterson Hensley
Clown	Michael Shawn Crahan
Joe Cocker	John Robert Cocker
Nat King Cole	Nathaniel Adams Coles
Common	Lonnie Rashid Lynn Jr
Coolio	Artis Ivey Jr
Alice Cooper	Vincent Damon Furnier
David Copperfield	David Kotkin
Dave 'Baby' Cortez	David Clowney
Elvis Costello	Declan Patrick McManus
Lou Costello	Louis Francis Cristillo
John Cougar	John Mellencamp
Lobo Courtney	Kent Lavoie
Joan Crawford	Lucille Le Sueur
Michael Crawford	Michael Dumble-Smith
Peter Criss	George Peter John Criscuola
Bing Crosby	Harry Lillis Crosby
Tom Cruise	Thomas Mapother IV
Ice Cube	O'Shea Jackson
Tony Curtis	Bernard Schwartz
Willie D	William James Dennis
Dick Dale	Richard Monsour

★ ★ ★ ★ REAL NAMES OF THE STARS ★ ★ ★ ★

Rodney Dangerfield	Jacob Cohen
Bobby Darin	Walden Robert Cassotto
Geena Davis	Virginia Elizabeth Davis
Doris Day	Doris von Kappelhoff
Jimmy Dean	Seth Ward
John Decon	John Richard Deacon
Joey Dee	Joseph DiNicola
Kiki Dee	Pauline Mathews
Sandra Dee	Alexandra Zuck
Mos Def	Dante Terrell Smith
John Denver	Henry John Deutschendorf Jr
Johnny Depp	John Christopher Depp II
John Derek	Derek Harris
Rick Derringer	Richard Zehringer
Danny DeVito	Daniel Michaeli
Buck Dharma	Donald Roeser
Angie Dickinson	Angeline Brown
Bo Diddley	Ellas Otha Bates
Dido	Florian Cloud de Bounevialle Armstrong
Vin Diesel	Mark Vincent
Snoop Dogg	Cordazer Calvin Broadus Jr
Mickey Dolenz	George Michael Braddock
Fats Domino	Antoine Domino
Donovan	Donovan Phillip Leitch
Diana Dors	Diana Fluck
Kirk Douglas	Issur Danielovitch

★ ★ ★ ★ REAL NAMES OF THE STARS ★ ★ ★ ★

Dr. Dre	Andre Young
Bob Dylan	Robert Alan Zimmerman

E

Easy E	Eric Wright
Sheila E.	Sheila Escovedo
Sheena Easton	Sheena Shirley Orr
Barbara Eden	Barbara Huffman
The Edge	David Howell Evans
Carmen Electra	Tara Patrick
Missy Elliot	Melissa Elliott
Eminem	Marshal Bruce Mathers III
Enya	Eithne Ni Braona
David Essex	David Albert Cook
Gloria Estefan	Gloria Maria Fajardo
Little Eva	Eva Narcissus Boyd
Don Everly	Isaac Donald Everly
Kenny Everett	Maurice Cole

F

Fabian	Fabiona Forte Bonaparte
Douglas Fairbanks	Douglas Ullman
Adam Faith	Terence Nelhams
Falco	Johann Hölzel
Tal Farlow	Talmage Holt Farlow

★ ★ ★ ★ REAL NAMES OF THE STARS ★ ★ ★ ★

Freddie Fender	Baldemar G. Huerta
Feist	Leslie Feist
Fergie	Stacy Ann Ferguson
(The Black Eyed Peas)	
Will Ferrell	John William Ferrell
Sally Field	Sally Mahoney
WC Fields	William Claude Dukenfield
Grandmaster Flash	Joseph Saddler
Flava Flav	William Jonathan Drayton Jr
Flea	Michael Peter Balzary
Joan Fontaine	Joan de Havilland
Jodie Foster	Alicia Christian Foster
Jamie Foxx	Eric Marlon Bishop
Black Francis (Pixies)	Charles Michael Kittridge Thompson IV
Connie Francis	Concetta Maria Franconero
Ace Frehley	Paul Daniel Frehley

G

Kenny G	Kenneth Gorelick
Greta Garbo	Greta Gustafsson
John Garfield	Julius Garfinkle
Judy Garland	Frances Gumm
Ginuwine	Elgin Lumpkin
Boy George	George Alan O'Dowd
Mel Gibson	Mel Columcille Gerard Gibson

★ ★ ★ ★ REAL NAMES OF THE STARS ★ ★ ★ ★

Gary Glitter	Paul Gadd
Whoopie Goldberg	Caryn Johnson
Goldie	Clifford Price
Cary Grant	Archibald Leach
Hugh Grant	Hugh John Mungo Grant
Macy Gray	Natalie Renee McIntyre

H

Gene Hackman	Eugene Allen Hackman
MC Hammer	Stanley Kirk Burrel
Jean Harlow	Harlean Carpentier
Woody Harrelson	Woodrow Tracy Harrelson
Ethan Hawke	Ethan Green Hawke
Rita Hayworth	Margarita Cansino
Jimi Hendrix	(born: Johnny Allen Hendrix) (renamed: James Marshall Hendrix)
Charlton Heston	John Charles Carter
Benny Hill	Alfred Hawthorne Hill
Faith Hill	Audrey Faith Perry
Hulk Hogan	Terry Jene Bollea
Billy Holiday	Eleanora Fagan
Judy Holliday	Judith Tuvim
Buddy Holly	Charles Hardin Holley
Bob Hope	Leslie Townes Hope
Leslie Howard	Leslie Stainer

★ ★ ★ ★ REAL NAMES OF THE STARS ★ ★ ★ ★

Harry Houdini	Ehrich Weiss
Rock Hudson	Roy Scherer Jr
Engelbert Humperdinck	Arnold George Dorsey

I

Janis Ian	Janis Eddy Fink
Vanilla Ice	Robert Van Winkle
Billy Idol	William Michael Albert Broad
Julio Iglesias	Julio Iglesias de la Cueva
Tony Iommi	Anthony Frank Iommi

J

Wolfman Jack	Robert Weston Smith
Tito Jackson	Toriano Adaryll Jackson
Jamelia	Jamelia Niela Davis
Rick James	James Ambrose Johnson Jr
David Jason	David John White
Jazz	Larry Anthony Jr
D.J. Jazzy Jeff	Jeffrey A Townes
Jewel	Jewel Kilcher
Billy Joel	William Joseph Martin Joel
Elton John	Reginald Kenneth Dwight
Don Johnson	Donald Wayne
Al Jolson	Asa Yoelson
Grace Jones	Grace Mendoza

★ ★ ★ ★ REAL NAMES OF THE STARS ★ ★ ★ ★

Jennifer Jones	Phyllis Isley
Tom Jones	Thomas Jones Woodward
Jordan	Katie Price
Wynonna Judd	Christina Claire Ciminella
Juvenile	Terius Grey

K

K.C.(of the Sunshine Band)	Harry Wayne Casey
Boris Karloff	William Henry Pratt
Kaskade	Ryan Raddon
R Kelly	Robert Kelly
The Great Kat	Katherine Thomas
Diane Keaton	Diane Hall
Alicia Keys	Alicia Augello Cook
Chaka Khan	Carole Yvette Marie Stevens
Nicole Kidman	Nicole Mary Kidman
Andy Kim	Andrew Youakim
Lil' Kim	Kimberly Jones
BB King	Riley B King
Larry King	Larry Zeigler
Ben Kingsley	Krishna Banji

L

Cheryl Ladd	Cheryl Stoppelmoor
Frankie Laine	Frankie LoVecchio

★ ★ ★ ★ REAL NAMES OF THE STARS ★ ★ ★ ★

Veronica Lake	Constance Ockleman
Michael Landon	Eugene Orowitz
kd lang	Kathryn Dawn Lang
Queen Latifah	Dana Owens
Cyndi Lauper	Cynthia Ann Stephanie Lauper
Stan Laurel	Arthur Jefferson
Jude Law	David Jude Heyworth Law
Steve Lawrence	Sidney Leibowitz
Heath Ledger	Heathcliff Andrew Ledger
Brenda Lee	Brenda Mae Tarpley
Geddy Lee	Gary Lee Weinrib
Gypsy Rose Lee	Rose Louise Hovick
Peggy Lee	Norma Deloris Egstrom
Janet Leigh	Jeanette Morrison
Julian Lennon	John Charles Julian Lennon
Huey Lewis	Hugh Anthony Cregg
Jerry Lewis	Joseph Levitch
Liberace	Wladziu Lee Valentino
Little Richard	Richard Penniman
LL Cool J	James Todd Smith
Professor Longhair	Henry Roeland Byrd
Sophia Loren	Sophia Scicoloni
Peter Lorre	Laszio Lowenstein
Courtney Love	Courtney Michelle Harrison
Ludacris	Christopher Brian Bridges
Béla Lugosi	Bela Ferenc Blasko

★ ★ ★ ★ REAL NAMES OF THE STARS ★ ★ ★ ★

Lulu	Marie McDonald McLaughlin Lawrie

M

M.I.A.	Mathangi Arulpragasam
Spanky MacFarlane	Elaine MacFarlane
Lonnie Mack	Lonnie McIntosh
Shirley MacLaine	Shirley Beatty
Elle Macpherson	Eleanor Gow
Madonna	Madonna Louise Veronica Ciccone
Tobey Maguire	Tobias Vincent Maguire
Taj Mahal	Henry St Clair Fredricks
Lee Majors	Harvey Lee Yeary II
Mama Cass Elliot	Ellen Naomi Cohen
Barry Manilow	Barry Alan Pincus
Manfred Mann	Manfred Lubowitz
Jayne Mansfield	Vera Jane Palmer
Marilyn Manson	Brian Hugh Warner
Mick Mars	Robert Alan Deal
Dean Martin	Dino Paul Crocetti
Ricky Martin	Enrique Jose Martin Morales
Dean Martin	Dino Crocetti
Chico Marx	Leonard Marx
Groucho Marx	Julius Marx
Gummo Marx	Milton Marx
Harpo Marx	Adolph Marx
Zeppo Marx	Herbert Marx

★ ★ ★ ★ REAL NAMES OF THE STARS ★ ★ ★ ★

Paul McCartney	James Paul McCartney
Roger McGuinn	James Joseph McGuinn III
Meat Loaf	Marvin Lee Aday
Freddie Mercury	Farrokh Bulsara
George Michael	Yorgos Panayiotou
Spike Milligan	Terence Alan Milligan
Joni Mitchell	Roberta Joan Anderson
Moby	Richard Melville Hall
Pharoahe Monch	Troy Donald Jamerson
Marilyn Monroe	Norma Jean Baker
Demi Moore	Demetria Gene Guynes
Garry Moore	Thomas Garrison Morfit
Julianne Moore	Julie Anne Smith
Van Morrison	George Ivan Morrison
Morrissey	Steven Patrick Morrissey
Mya	Mya Harrison
Mystikal	Michael Tyler

N

Nas	Nasir Jones
Sam Neill	Nigel John Dermot Neill
Nelly	Carnell Haynes Jr
Rick Nelson	Eric Hilliard Nelson
Nico	Christa Paffgen
Nilsson	Harry Edward Nilsson III
Noodles	Kevin Wasserman

★ ★ ★ ★ REAL NAMES OF THE STARS ★ ★ ★ ★

Chuck Norris	Carlos Ray
Notorious B.I.G.	Christopher Wallace
Kim Novak	Marilyn Pauline Novak
Gary Numan	Gary Anthony James Webb

O

Billy Ocean	Leslie Sebastian Charles
Gary Oldman	Leonard Gary Oldman
Roy Orbison	Roy Kelton Orbison
Tony Orlando	Michael Anthony Orlando Cassivitis
Benjamin Orr	Benjamin Orzechowski
George Orwell	Eric Blair
Ozzy Osbourne	John Michael Osbourne
Gilbert O'Sullivan	Raymond Edward O'Sullivan

P

P Diddy	Sean John Combs
Patti Page	Clara Ann Fowler
Jack Palance	Walter Palanuik
Robert Palmer	Alan Batley
Robert Palmer	Alan Robert Palmer
Gram Parsons	Cecil Ingram Connor, III
Gregory Peck	Eldred Gregory Peck
Pepa (Salt-n-Pepa)	Sandra Denton

★ ★ ★ ★ REAL NAMES OF THE STARS ★ ★ ★ ★

Bernadette Peters	Bernadette Lazzaro
Lou Diamond Phillips	Lou Upchurch
Slim Pickens	Louis Lindley
Mary Pickford	Gladys Smith
Pink	Alecia Moore
Brad Pitt	William Bradley Pitt
Iggy Pop	James Newell Osterberg Jr
Janet Street Porter	Janet Bull
Natalie Portman	Natalie Hershlag
Stephanie Powers	Stefania Federkiewicz
Maxi Priest	Max Elliot
Prince	Prince Rogers Nelson

R

CJ Ramone	Chris Ward
Dee Dee Ramone	Douglas Colvin
Joey Ramone	Jeffery Hyman
Johnny Ramone	John Cummings
Marky Ramone	Mark Bell
Richie Ramone	Richie Reinhart
Tommy Ramone	Tom Erdelyi
Dizzee Rascal	Dylan Mills
Martha Raye	Margaret Theresa Yvonne Reed
Donna Reed	Donna Belle Mullenger
Lou Reed	Louis Firbank
Vic Reeves	Jim Moir

★ ★ ★ ★ REAL NAMES OF THE STARS ★ ★ ★ ★

Busta Rhymes	Trevor Tahiem Smith
Cliff Richard	Harry Roger Webb
Little Richard	Richard Wayne Penniman
Joan Rivers	Joan Sandra Molinsky
Smokey Robinson	William Robinson
Edward G Robinson	Emmanuel Goldenberg
Rihanna	Robyn Rihanna Fenty
Ginger Rogers	Virginia McMath
Roy Rogers	Leonard Slye
Henry Rollins	Henry Garfield
Mickey Rooney	Joe Yule Jr
Axl Rose	(born: William Bruce Rose Jr) (renamed: William Bailey)
Johnny Rotten	John Joseph Lydon
Ja Rule	Jeffery Atkins
Meg Ryan	Margaret Mary Emily Anne Hyra
Winona Ryder	Winona Horowitz

S

Sade	Helen Folasade Adu
Telly Savalas	Aristotelis Harris Savalas
Leo Sayer	Gerald Hugh Sayer
Seal	Henry Olusegun Olumide Samuel
Peter Sellers	Richard Henry Sellers

★ ★ ★ ★ REAL NAMES OF THE STARS ★ ★ ★ ★

Jane Seymour	Joyce Frankenberg
Shaggy	Orville Richard Burrell
Shakira	Shakira Isabel Mebarak Ripoll
Omar Sharif	Michael Shalhoub
Charlie Sheen	Carlos Irwin Estevez
Gene Simmons	Chaim Klein Witz
Nina Simone	Eunice Wayman
Nikki Sixx	Franklin Carlton Serafino Feranna
Frank Skinner	Chris Collins
Slash	Saul Hudson
Christian Slater	Christian Michael Leonard Hawkins
Grace Slick	Grace Barnett Wing
Fatboy Slim	Quentin Cook (aka Norman Cook)
Patti Smith	Patricia Lee Smith
Anna Nicole Smith	Vickie Lynn Hogan
Sissy Spacek	Mary Elizabeth Spacek
Kevin Spacey	Kevin John Fowler
Baby Spice	Emma Lee Bunton
Ginger Spice	Geraldine Estelle Halliwell
Posh Spice	Victoria Caroline Beckham
Scary Spice	Melanie Janine Brown
Sporty Spice	Melanie Jayne Chisholm
Dusty Springfield	Mary Isabel Catherine Bernadette O'Brien

★ ★ ★ ★ REAL NAMES OF THE STARS ★ ★ ★ ★

Sylvester Stallone	Sylvester Gardenzio
Freddie Starr	Freddie Powell
Ringo Starr	Richard Starkey
Cat Stevens	Steven Demetre Georgiou (1979, became Yusuf Islam)
Shakin Stevens	Michael Barratt
Sting	Gordon Matthew Thomas Sumner
Michael Stipe	John Michael Stipe
Angie Stone	Angela Laverne Brown
Joss Stone	Joscelyn Eve Stocker
Sly Stone	Sylvester Stewart
Meryl Streep	Mary Louise Streep
Joe Strummer	John Graham Mellor
Suggs	Graham McPherson
Donna Summer	LaDonna Adrian Gaines
Sun Ra	Herman Poole Blount

T

Booker T	Booker T Jones
Ice T	Tracy Marrow
Taboo	Jaime Luis Gómez
David Tennant	David McDonald
Billy Bob Thornton	William Robert Thornton
Johnny Thunders	John Anthony Genzale Jr
Timbaland	Timothy Z Mosley

★ ★ ★ ★ REAL NAMES OF THE STARS ★ ★ ★ ★

Tina Turner	Annie Mae Bullock
Shania Twain	Eilleen Regina Edwards
Twiggy	Leslie Hornby
Bonnie Tyler	Gaynor Hopkins
Steven Tyler	Steven Victor Tallarico

U

Usher	Usher Raymond
Peter Ustinov	Peter Alexander von Ustinow

V

Frankie Valli	Frank Castelluccio
Jean-Claude Van Damme	Jean-Claude Camille François Van Varenberg
Eddie Vedder	Edward Louis Severson III
Tom Verlaine	Thomas Miller
Sid Vicious	John Simon Ritchie
Gene Vincent	Vincent Craddock
Vinnie Vincent	Vincent Cusano

W

Christopher Walken	Ronald Walken
David Walliams	David Williams
Andy Warhol	Andrew Warhola

★ ★ ★ ★ REAL NAMES OF THE STARS ★ ★ ★ ★

Dionne Warwick	Marie Dionne Warwick
John Wayne	Marion Michael Morrison
Sigourney Weaver	Susan Alexandra Weaver
Raquel Welch	Raquel Tejada
Kanye West	Kanye Omari West
Jack White	John Anthony Gillis
Kim Wilde	Kim Smith
Gene Wilder	Jerome Silberman
Bruce Willis	Walter Willison
Will.i.am	William James Adams Jr
Hank Williams	Hiram Williams
Barbara Windsor	Barbara-Ann Deeks
Kate Winslet	Katherine Elizabeth Winslet
Shelley Winters	Shirley Schrift
Nicky Wire	Nicholas Allen Jones
Reese Witherspoon	Laura Jeanne Reese Witherspoon
Howlin' Wolf	Chester Arthur Burnett
Stevie Wonder	(born: Steveland Hardaway Judkins) (renamed: Steveland Hardaway Morris)
Natalie Wood	Natalia Nikolaevna Zakharenko
Lil Bow Wow	Shad Anthony Moss
Bill Wyman	William Perks
Jane Wyman	Sarah Jane Fulks
Tammy Wynette	Virginia Wynette Pugh

★ ★ ★ ★ REAL NAMES OF THE STARS ★ ★ ★ ★

Y

Yazz   Yasmin Evans

Z

Robin Zander   Robin Wayne Zander
Frank Zappa   Frank Vincent Zappa
Dweezil Zappa   Ian Donald Calvin Euclid
                            Zappa
Catherine Zeta Jones   Catherine Jones

THE NAME GAME – THE CRAZIEST BABY NAMES IN THE WORLD

★ ★ ★ ★ THE CRAZIEST BABY NAMES IN THE WORLD ★ ★ ★ ★

A

Ace	Nicole Appleton and Liam Howlett
Adria	Tom Petty
Agnes	Thom Yorke
Ahmet Emuukha Roden	Frank Zappa
Aja Louise	Mitch Dorge
Alabama Luella	Travis Barker and Shanna Moakler
Alaia	Stephen Baldwin
Alessandra	Andy Garcia
Alexa	Troy Aikman
Alexa Rae	Billy Joel and Christie Brinkley
Alfonso	Morgan Freeman
Alisabeth	Tyne Daly
Allegra Sky	John Leguizamo
Alyxandra	Tyne Daly
Amandine	John Malkovich
Amba	Jade Jagger
Amber Rose	Simon and Yasmin Le Bon
Aminta	Pete Townshend
Anais	Noel Gallagher and Meg Mathews
Annaliza	Steven Seagal and Kelly Lebrock
Anton	Al Pacino and Beverly D'Angelo
Apple	Gwyneth Paltrow and Chris

★ ★ ★ ★ THE CRAZIEST BABY NAMES IN THE WORLD ★ ★ ★ ★

Martin Aquinnah	Michael J Fox and Tracy Pollan
Arpad Flynn	Elle Macpherson
Arrisa	Steven Seagal and Kelly Lebrock
Arun	The Edge
Assisi	Jade Jagger
Astrella Celeste	Donovan
Atherton Grace	Don Johnson
Atlanta Noo	John Taylor and Amanda De Cadenet
Atticus	Tony Adams
Auden	Noah Wyle
Audice	Adrian Belew
Audio Science	Shannyn Sossaman
Aurelius Cy	Elle Macpherson
Autumn	Forest Whitaker
Avalon	Mike Kroeger

B

Beau Devin	David Cassidy
Bebe Orleans	Nuno Bettencourt
Bechet Dumaine	Woody Allen and Soon-Yi Previn
Beckett	Malcolm McDowell
Bella	Billy Bob Thornton
Betty Kitten	Jonathan Ross and Jane Goldman
Bibi Belle	Anna Ryder Richardson

★ ★ ★ ★ THE CRAZIEST BABY NAMES IN THE WORLD ★ ★ ★ ★

Blossom	Kacey Ainsworth
Blue Angel	The Edge
Bo	Ulrika Jonsson
Bobbi Kristina	Bobby Brown and Whitney Houston
Bobby Jack	Jade Goody and Jeff Brazier
Bonnie Blue	Billy Idol
Boston	Kurt Russell
Brandi	Roseanne Barr
Brawley	Nick Nolte
Bria	Eddie Murphy
Brooklyn	David and Victoria Beckham
Bruno	Nigella Lawson
Buck	Roseanne Barr

C

Caleb	Jack Nicholson
Caley Leigh	Chevy Chase
Cali Tee	James Hetfield
Calico	Alice Cooper
Calista	David Carradine
Carmen	Robert Plant
Carnie	Brian Wilson
Cash	Slash
Cashel Blake	Daniel Day-Lewis
Caspar	Claudia Schiffer and Matthew Vaughn

★ ★ ★ ★ THE CRAZIEST BABY NAMES IN THE WORLD ★ ★ ★ ★

Cassius	Damien Hirst
Castor Virgil	James Hetfield
Chadwick	Steve McQueen
Chanel	Nelly
Chianna Maria	Sonny and Mary Bono
Chastity	Cher and Sonny Bono
Chudney	Diana Ross
Clementine	Claudia Schiffer and Matthew Vaughn
Coco Riley	Courtney Cox and David Arquette
Cooper Philip	Seymour Hoffman
Corde	Snoop Dogg
Cordell	Snoop Dogg
Corey	Suzanne Shaw and Darren Day
Cori	Snoop Dog
Cosima	Nigella Lawson
Cross	Big Boi from OutKast
Cruz	Victoria and David Beckham
Cydney Cathalene	Chevy Chase

D

Daisy Boo	Jamie Oliver
Dakota Mayi	Don Johnson and Melanie Griffith
Damian	Liz Hurley and Steve Bing
Dandelion	Keith Richards

★ ★ ★ ★ THE CRAZIEST BABY NAMES IN THE WORLD ★ ★ ★ ★

Dashiell	Cate Blanchett
Deacon	Reese Witherspoon
Deena	Morgan Freeman
Deni Montana	Woody Harrelson
Denim	Toni Braxton
Destry	Steven Spielberg and Kate Capshaw
Deva	Monica Bellucci
Dexter	Diana Keaton
Dhani	George Harrison
Diezel	Toni Braxton
Dilyn	Nicole Eggert
Diva Muffin	Frank Zappa
Domenica	Martin Scorsese
Duke	Diana Keaton
Dusti Rain	Vanilla Ice
Dweezil	Frank Zappa
Dylan Jagger	Pamela Anderson and Tommy Lee

E

Eja	Shania Twain and Robert John Lange
Eliana	Christian Slater
Elijah Blue	Cher and Greg Allman
Elijah Patricius Bob	Bono Guggi Q
Ella Bleu	John Travolta and Kelly Preston

★ ★ ★ ★ THE CRAZIEST BABY NAMES IN THE WORLD ★ ★ ★ ★

Emerson	Teri Hatcher
Esme	Anthony Edwards
Eugenie	Prince Andrew and Sarah Ferguson
Eulala	Marcia Gay Harden
Evie	Sean Bean
Ezekiel	Beau Bridges

F

Fifi Trixibelle	Bob Geldof and Paula Yates
Finlay	Sadie Frost and Gary Kemp
Free	David Carradine and Barbara Hershey

G

Gabriel Luke Beauregard	Mick Jagger and Jerry Hall
Gabriel-Kane	Daniel Day-Lewis
Gabriel Wilk	Mia Farrow
Gaia	Emma Thompson
Galen Grier	Dennis Hopper
Gene	Liam Gallagher and Nicole Appleton
Geronimo	Alex James
Giacomo	Sting
Greer	Kelsey Grammer
Griffin	Brendan Fraser
Gulliver	Gary Oldman

★ ★ ★ ★ THE CRAZIEST BABY NAMES IN THE WORLD ★ ★ ★ ★

H

Hailie	Eminem and Kim Mathers
Happy	Macy Gray
Harlow	Patricia Arquette
Harvey Kirby	Jonathan Ross and Jane Goldman
Heavenly Hiraani Tiger Lily	Paula Yates and Michael Hutchence
Homer	Richard Gere
Honey Kinney	Jonathan Ross and Jane Goldman
Hopper Jack	Robin Wright Penn

I

Indiana August	Casey Affleck and Summer Phoenix
Indio	Robert Downey Jr
Ireland	Kim Basinger and Alec Baldwin
Iris	Sadie Frost and Jude Law
Isadora	Björk
Iset	Wesley Snipes

J

Jade Sheena Jezebel	Mick and Bianca Jagger
Jaden Christopher Syre	Will Smith and Jada Pinkett Smith

★ ★ ★ ★ THE CRAZIEST BABY NAMES IN THE WORLD ★ ★ ★ ★

Jakob	Bob Dylan
Jaya	R Kelly
Jenna	Dustin Hoffman
Jermajesty	Jermaine Jackson
Jersey	Nicky Butt
Jessamine	Paul Weller
Jesse James	Jon Bon Jovi
Jett	John Travolta and Kelly Preston
Jones	Cerys Matthews
Jourdyn	Jermaine Jackson
Jude	Mackenzie Crook
Junior Savva	Katie Price and Peter Andre

K

Kai	Jennifer Connelly
Kaia Jordan	Cindy Crawford and Rande Gerber
Kaiis	Geena Davis
Kailand	Stevie Wonder
Kal-El	Nicolas Cage
Kaleb	Kevin Federline
Kansas	David Carradine
Karis	Mick Jagger and Marsha Hunt
Karsen	Ray Liotta
Katia	Denzel Washington
Kecalf	Aretha Franklin
Kian	Geena Davis

★ ★ ★ ★ THE CRAZIEST BABY NAMES IN THE WORLD ★ ★ ★ ★

Kit	Jodie Foster
Kyd	David Duchovny and Tea Leoni

L

Laird Vonne	Sharon Stone
Landon	Bobby Brown
Langston	Laurence Fishburne
Laprincia	Bobby Brown
Lark Song	Mia Farrow
Leni	Heidi Klum and Flavio Briatore
Lennon	Liam Gallagher and Patsy Kensit
Levi	The Edge
Levon Room	Uma Thurman and Ethan Hawke
Liberty	Ryan Giggs
Lila Grace	Kate Moss and Jefferson Hack
Lily-Rose Melody	Johnny Depp and Vanessa Paradis
Lilyella	Melanie Blatt
Loewy	John Malkovich
Lola	Sara Cox and Jon Carter
Lola Simone	Chris Rock
London Emilio	Slash
Lourdes Maria	Madonna

★ ★ ★ ★ THE CRAZIEST BABY NAMES IN THE WORLD ★ ★ ★ ★

Luca	Colin Firth and Livia Giugglioni
Lucian	Steve Buscemi
Lulu	Paul Simon and Edie Bricknell
Luna	Frank Lampard
Lux	Bobby Gillespie

M

Mackenzie	JK Rowling
Maddox	Angelina Jolie and Billy Bob Thornton
Makena'lei	Helen Hunt
Mandisa	Danny Glover
Mandla Kadjay Carl	Stevie Wonder
Manzie Tio	Woody Allen and Soon-Yi Previn
Marina Pearl	Matt Leblanc and Melissa Mc Knight
Marquise	50 Cent
Martha Sky Hope	Ulrika Jonsson
Mason	Kelsey Grammer
Mateo	Colin Firth and Livia Giuggioli
Mateo Braverly	Banjamin Bratt and Talisa Soto
Maya	Uma Thurman and Ethan Hawke

★ ★ ★ ★ THE CRAZIEST BABY NAMES IN THE WORLD ★ ★ ★ ★

Max Liron	Christina Aguilera and Jordan Bratman
Memphis	Bono
Mercedes	Val Kilmer and Joanne Whalley
Mikaela	Steven Spielberg and Kate Capshaw
Miller	Stella McCartney
Milo	Liv Tyler
Mingus	Helena Christensen
Missy	Damon Albarn
Misty Kid	Sharleen Spiteri
Moon Unit	Frank Zappa
Morgan	Clint Eastwood
Morgana	Morgan Freeman
Moses Amadeus	Woody Allen and Mia Farrow

N

Navarone	Priscilla Presley
Nell Marmalade	Helen Baxendale
Nevis	Nelly Furtado
Noah	Thom Yorke

O

Ocean	Forest Whitaker

P

Paige Carlyle	Ron Howard

★ ★ ★ ★ The crAziest bAby nAmes in the world ★ ★ ★ ★

Paloma	Emilio Estevez
Paris Michael	Michael Jackson and Debbie Rowe
Parker	Fay Ripley
Peaches Honeyblossom	Bob Geldof and Paula Yates
Pearl	Meat Loaf
Pedro	Frances McDormand and Joel Coen
Pepper	Graham Coxon
Persia	Gary Numan
Phinnaeus	Julia Roberts and Danny Moder
Phoenix Chi	Mel B
Pilot Inspecktor	Jason Lee
Piper Maru	Gillian Anderson
Pixie	Bob Geldof and Paula Yates
Poppy Honey	Jamie Oliver
Presley	Cindy Crawford and Rande Gerber
Prince Michael	Michael Jackson and Debbie Rowe
Prince Michael II	Michael Jackson and Debbie Rowe

Q

Quinlan	Ben Stiller

★ ★ ★ ★ THE CRAZIEST BABY NAMES IN THE WORLD ★ ★ ★ ★

R

Racer	Robert Rodriguez
Rafe	Timothy Spall
Rafferty	Jude Law and Sadie Frost
Rain	Richard Pryor
Rainey	Andie MacDowell
Raphael	Robert De Niro
Raven	Gary Numan
Rebop	Todd Rundgren
Redmond	Farrah Fawcett and Ryan O'Neal
Regan	Paul Gascoigne and Sheryl Kyle
Renee	Rod Stewart and Rachel Hunter
Roan	Sharon Stone
Rocco	Madonna and Guy Ritchie
Roeg	Donald Sutherland
Roman	Cate Blanchett
Romeo	David and Victoria Beckham
Rumer Glenn	Demi Moore and Bruce Willis
Ryder Russell	Kate Hudson and Chris Robinson

S

Saifoulaye	Morgan Freeman
Sage Moonblood	Sylvester Stallone

★ ★ ★ ★ THE CRAZIEST BABY NAMES IN THE WORLD ★ ★ ★ ★

Salome	Alex Kingston
Satchel	Woody Allen and Mia Farrow
Sawyer	Steven Spielberg and Kate Capshaw
Schuyler	Michael J Fox
Scout La Rue	Demi Moore and Bruce Willis
Sean Preston	Britney Spears and Kevin Federline
Shauna	Robert Redford
Shavaar	Ms Dynamite
Shepherd Kellen	Jerry Seinfeld
Sindri	Björk
Sonnet	Forest Whitaker
Sosie	Kevin Bacon and Kyra Sedgwick
Stellan	Jenifer Connelly and Paul Bettany
Summer Song	Mia Farrow

T

Tallulah Belle	Demi Moore and Bruce Willis
Tallulah Lilac	Jessie Wallace
Travis	Kevin Bacon and Kyra Sedgwick
True Isabella Summer	Forest Whitaker
Truman	Tom Hanks

★ ★ ★ ★ **THE CRAZIEST BABY NAMES IN THE WORLD** ★ ★ ★ ★

V

Valentino Luca	Melanie Sykes

W

Weston	Nicolas Cage
Willard	Will Smith
Willem Wolfe	Billy Idol
Willow Camille Reign	Will Smith and Jada Pinkett Smith
Woody	Zoe Ball and Norman Cook
Wyatt	Kurt Russell and Goldie Hawn

Z

Zahara Marley	Angelina Jolie
Zelda	Robin Williams
Zola	Eddie Murphy
Zowie	David Bowie